THE PRACTICAL CAMP COOK

FRED BOUWMAN

Second Printing: May, 1998

International Standard Book Number:
0-88290-328-4

Horizon Publishers' Catalog and Order Number:
1237

Printed and Distributed
in the United States of America by

Horizon Publishers
& Distributors, Incorporated

Mailing Address:
P.O. Box 490
Bountiful, Utah 84011-0490

Street Address:
50 South 500 West
Bountiful, Utah 84010

Local Phone: (801) 295-9451
Toll free: 1 (866) 818-6277
FAX: (801) 295-0196

E-mail: horizonp@burgoyne.com
Internet Home Page: http://www.horizonpublishers.biz

Contents

1

Meat

The meal I remember best, of all of them I've eaten in camps over the years, is the tenderloins, liver and heart of a big doe Dale took back in the pines by the river. In camp that night the fire flickered and snapped under the northern lights. It was chilly, with a promise of snow, and we watched the steam and smoke rising from blackened, dented cook pots and pans on the grate over the fire pit. There was lots of laughter as we ate real meat that night.

We ate no venison the next season, but a squirrel-and-rabbit stew took honors as the meal that would be recalled long after the memory of the rest of the hunt had faded.

From overnight single-tent camps huddled beside diminutive northern lakes, to mosquito-bitten spring turkey hunting camps, to camps on sand bars with the Wisconsin River sucking and gurgling on either side, to large-scale tent camps pitched on a blanket of deer hunter's snow at the end of a National Forest logging road, the trend in our outdoor menus has been away from the supermarket. We've moved towards eating "off the land" as much as the situation allows. And though gathering wild plant foods figures in during most any time of the year, a good number of our camp meals feature wild meat.

The explorer Vilhjalmur Stefansson spent five years living among primitive Eskimos above the arctic circle. For months on end Stefansson and his companions subsisted on raw meat and seal fat. They flourished.

Straight meat diets require quite some deviance from our accustomed eating habits. For instance, the pre-white-era Eskimo diet included all of the seal, caribou, or whatever from bone marrow to

A complete camp meal, with meat as the main course.

such aboriginal culinary delights as stomach contents to obtain the complete nutrition offered by an animal, which is more than most of us are willing to indulge in around the fire during deer or grouse season.

Meat—A Source of Complete Nourishment

Though milk from domestic cattle is sometimes billed as "nature's perfect food," that label can be more properly applied to meat. Unlike any other single class of foods, a diet of fat red meat, either raw or cooked rare enough as to not destroy the vitamin C, will support life without any additional supplement.

Not only is wild game meat capable of providing complete nourishment for humans, but game meats themselves, from a venison roast to duck, are better for you than their domestic counterparts. Fat content is the main culprit--domestic meat animals are loaded with it in comparison to wild game.

From the United States Department of Agriculture publication Composition of Foods, let's compare the protein and fat content of some wild game animals and their tame cousins:

*There is no more appropriate place to enjoy
venison steaks than over the fire in camp.*

	Protein	Fat
	(Grams per pound)	
Venison	95	18
Beef	67.3	97.1
Rabbit--wild	76	18
Rabbit--domestic	75	29
Duck--wild	55.5	41.6
Duck--domestic	47.2	84.3

As you can see, wild meat holds the edge by a healthy (pun intended) margin in the area of reducing fat in the diet. In addition, wild animals are devoid of the antibiotics and growth-enhancement drug residues encountered in domestic animal meats.

of course, this type of diet can raise problems. Uncooked or undercooked game meats may transfer disease or parasites. I include the above statement on the nutritional value of meat only to illustrate its compatibility with human nutritional needs, and not as a "plug" for an all meat raw foods diet.

Too many camp meat menus never get past the point of burgers broiled over the fire. Even deer and elk camps, which may have several hundred pounds of meat hanging, often fail to utilize any of it until the butcher sends it back wrapped in paper or plastic.

Enjoy Small Game Too

The tenderloins, liver, and heart supper mentioned at the beginning of this chapter is a good one to begin expanding your natural foods diet, but there are other possibilities.

Small game is a natural for camp. Ducks barbecued over an open fire can't be improved on in the home kitchen. If there's a Dutch oven with a little rice, and a few grouse over that same fire, it will turn into a meal guaranteed to be the high point of the trip.

Before we go any further, let me stress that the point of this book is not to make bringing food to camp obsolete. With the possible exception of some big game hunts, to supply oneself exclusively with meat, fish, or plant foods taken in the field is often either illegal, unethical, or both. There just isn't that much food out there in these crowded times.

A few traps placed around your camp can supply a new source of menu choices.

Wise use of what nature offers, however, is another matter entirely. In addition to the usual "game" animals, there are a number of other edible forest denizens that are legal to take. They can be eaten without worrying about depleting the resource and they're quite tasty.

"And do not despise the fretful porcupine, he is better than he looks," wrote George Washington Sears, the early twentieth-century naturalist and outdoorsman who wrote under the pseudonym

"Nessmuk." Sears lived in the days when one would hit the foot and canoe portage trail with a sack of flour or cornmeal, some salt, and a chunk of slab bacon or salt pork. Meat was procured as it was happened upon, without discussion of its qualities at table.

A partial list of perfectly edible animals includes the porcupine, opossum, raccoon, woodchuck, beaver, and muskrat, in addition to the common game animals like the grouse or rabbit. Folks who are brave enough to eat one claim that skunks are edible. I don't know. Coot, or mud hens, are fine eating if prepared properly. Foxes are edible but are too closely related to Lassie for most folk's tastes.

A pair of small traps adds to the meat supply in camp. Make sure to check state trapping regulations first.

The camper adding some wild protein to his menu will have to take local game laws into account. Some of the above-mentioned entrees are not considered game animals and will either carry no restrictions on their taking or will have very liberal seasons. Fur bearers can only be taken with traps in some states, and you may be required to have a trapping license to legally possess them. Know your game laws.

A string of half a dozen traps set around camp can provide a steady flow of exotic camp foods. Animals a trapper would consider "trash," due to their negligible monetary value, such as the porky or possum, are more than welcome in the Dutch oven or on a spit, with barbecue sauce. our few traps set around camp during the deer hunt provide variety to the camp menu, an opportunity to do some real gourmet outdoor cooking, and a sense of adventure about the evening meals.

Cleaning and Cooling Wild Meat in the Field

Much—perhaps too much—has been written on the care of wild game meat in the field. What essentially should be a simple exercise in common sense has been written and talked about to death. Bleeding or not bleeding, skinning or not skinning, washing or not washing, hanging or not hanging, and so forth have been discussed frequently. No matter what the wild diner does to ready his game for supper, someone will say that it's wrong.

If you perform a minimum of two simple tasks you have done an adequate job in caring for your game meat. First, clean the animal immediately. There should be no leaving it around in rubberized game bags or lying in the bottom of the boat. It's dead, and the moment an animal dies it begins to deteriorate. Managing this deterioration is the key to proper game meat care.

Second, cool it. Carry your dinner back to camp outside of your clothing, not stuffed in a pocket. Keep the animal out of direct sunlight, pack some snow into the abdominal cavity, do whatever you can at the time to lower the temperature of the meat.

But don't cool your venison the way one Wisconsin hunter did. An acquaintance of mine owns a small locker plant in rural northern Wisconsin and does a good business processing deer and an

Proper field care includes cooling the carcass as quickly as possible. Here snow is being placed in the cavity.

occasional bear during and after the season. He put a good-sized buck up on the band saw one year and promptly ruined the circular blade. Questioning the hunter brought to light the fact that the deer had been cooled after field dressing by laying it belly-up in a small, running stream. The current ran into the chest cavity where the resulting water turbulence caused sand and silt to settle in the deer and to work its way between the grains of the meat. Not only was an expensive saw blade lost, but much of the deer was inedible.

Perhaps the least-understood facet of caring for wild meat is the subject of aging, and here we will deviate from the teachings of the "old guys"- the beans, bacon, and bannock cookbook writers of the last century and the first half of this one. Myself, and the majority of the readers of this book, have been brought up eating grocery store meat. The term "meat-eating" in our grandparents' day meant either domestic meats without much of the refrigerated handling that they receive today, or in some cases game meats.

The moment an animal dies it begins to decompose, and we eat that meat at a stage of decomposition somewhere between alive and putrefaction, depending on the culture in which we have been brought up. Aging of meat is accomplished by the action of enzymes on the tissues and the action of bacteria. Some of these are normally found in the meat while others are picked up in the process of dressing or transporting it. These enzymes and bacteria break the meat down and change the flavor.

The beef you purchase at the grocery store meat counter will most likely have been dead less than a week at the time you carry it through the checkout. Premium-aged beef steaks ordered in a restaurant will have aged from ten days to perhaps three weeks. This aging process has taken place after the animal has been killed under sanitary conditions and has been immediately dressed. And the aging will have taken place in a refrigerated workplace. Many of the cuts are packaged in airtight, nitrogen-gas-flushed, plastic bags and transported under refrigerated conditions.

Contrast this to the normal hunting situation in which a deer, bird, or small game animal is taken. The animal is usually in a state of intense excitement at the time of death, which chemically detracts from the quality of the meat. Field dressing, even when carefully done by skillful hunters, still leaves the inside of the carcass contaminated with blood, intestinal and Fecal Cal matter, plus bacteria from the ground, the hunter's hands, knife blades, and any other object that comes into contact with the carcass during this process. The animal often is dragged along the ground, picking up more bacteria, and then hung. Even if it is wrapped in an insect-proof net, further bacterial contamination is probable.

Your best bet is to make no attempt to age wild garnet whether it be venison or small game or birds. You will attain the best-tasting wild game meats by taking a carcass from the kill site to the freezer or cook pot as quickly as possible, allowing little time for the bacteria on the meat to multiply and cause the "Barney" taste that actually isn't the taste of game at all. The finest farm-raised beef would taste the same if you treated it like wild game meats are usually treated.

Removing Scent Glands

Most animals do a good deal of their communicating by means of scent. They have specialized glands located at various places on their bodies which excrete fluids to produce these scents. The skunk is by far the most blatant example of this type of non-verbal communication, but all animals (including humans, according to some authorities) communicate to some degree in this manner.

Most of the literature is pretty vague on the subject of removing scent glands before cooking, and removing the glands without exercising some caution can cause more trouble than it prevents. Touching the gland itself with the hands while removing it, and then touching either the meat or cutting tools or surfaces, will endow your dinner with at best a "Barney" flavor. At worst it will make it inedible.

The scent glands familiar to many hunters are the metatarsal glands of the whitetail, located just below the knee joint on the insides of the rear legs. There will often be a rust-colored patch of hair below the glands, where the fluid has been secreted. Though a field dressing guide or one of the "old bucks" around camp may suggest removing these glands, I've never met a hunter who does, nor have I encountered any problems from leaving them in. If you can keep from touching them while skinning, or really do a thorough job of hand washing if you do touch the glands, you won't ever have any trouble.

Let's locate the glands on some animals that have to be removed and keep it simple. The glands you're looking for are the size of a kernel of corn. The woodchuck, possum, and beaver scent glands, up to nine of them per animal, are located under the forelegs and in the small of the back, and those of the muskrat are in the abdomen. Cut away an inch or so of flesh around the genitals when cleaning a beaver or muskrat. The glands on a raccoon are located underneath the forelegs and back of each hind leg.

other than the of these glands, all small animals can be cleaned and readied for cooking in about the same way. Squirrels and rabbits are easily skinned by cutting them across the back, then inserting the fingers of both hands and pulling the hide towards the head and tail simultaneously until it reaches the head and tail, at which point the hide pieces are cut off.

Skinning Small Animals and Birds

Other small animals can also be handled with a simple, quick procedure. Trappers have their own methods of skinning each animal, designed with the value of the hide in mind. For our purpose, which is a meal, suspend the animal by the hind feet, cut through the hide around the "ankles" of all four legs, cut through the hide from each rear leg to the anus, and then peel it. Slit the belly to remove the entrails and the hard part is done.

Cleaning birds is as simple as cleaning mammals, with the exception of the plucking versus skinning debate. Certain birds, particularly fish eaters such as the coot, should be skinned. The surface fat that is removed during the skinning holds the great majority of the fish taste that prevents many outdoorsmen from even bringing these birds home.

Any bird can be skinned, if you so wish, with the advantage that it requires only a fraction of the time you would need to pluck the bird. on the negative side of skinning is the fact that without exercising a great amount of care during the cooking process of a skinned bird, the meat will lose much of its juices, resulting in a dryer, lesser-quality dish.

With the exception of fish ducks, which should be skinned (because skinning them removes much of the fat layer which contains the fishy taste in these birds), plucking is required to get the most flavor from game birds as the skin seals in fat and other moisture. Plucking game birds is, quite frankly, boring, so let's look at the fastest way to accomplish the job.

Dry-plucking is the simplest way to remove a bird's feathers, but it takes the longest.

The original, time-tested method is just to pull out the feathers with your fingers. Its simple enough, and this works okay if the bird is warm. Pull "against the grain" for the best results.

If the bird has been sitting for a few hours after being shot, as is usually the case, dry-plucking changes from mere tedium to a truly diabolical exercise in mental torture. No matter how many feathers you get with each pull, there are still a few left, tickling the tips of your fingers. You'll never get done.

Upland birds should be scalded--put in and out of a pot of boiling water until the feathers begin to loosen, at which point plucking can commence. Waterfowl, with their oiled feathers, respond best to the paraffin treatment. Melt a pound or two of paraffin in a container of

Hot water and paraffin speeds up the plucking process.

water and dip the whole bird in the water. Upon drawing the bird out the paraffin, floating on the water, will coat the feathers. After cooling the bird, pulling the paraffin off in layers will bring feathers with it. Most birds will require two immersions, and geese call fora good sized container and several blocks of paraffin, but this method works so well that there is just no other route to go.

Removing the Entrails

Remove the entrails by making an incision from the anus to the breast, or cut off the entire tail section, and pull the entrails out as you would for any animal. The skin will usually peel easily on the fish ducks that you bring home. Just get your thumbs or fingers underneath it and work it off.

A look at the pocketknife of an old time waterfowler or upland bird gunner reveals a tool that won't be recognized by the sons and daughters of the old guys. The gut hook is just that. Its inserted into the vent of a bagged bird, a quick twist and pull are made, and much of the entrails are removed. The merit of this idea is open to debate: removing part of the entrails in this manner causes more internal bleeding.

Venison Tenderloin--The Traditional Deer-camp Feast

For deer hunters, a good starting point for expanding your outdoor menu possibilities is the heart, liver, and tenderloin dinner that to this day is an old family hunting tradition in many parts of the United States. But like family deer camps, canvas tents, and knee-high lace up leather boots, it is rapidly disappearing in these times of quick overnight or day-long hunting trips and motels. Enjoying a meal of this type will provide your camp with one of the finest meals you will ever enjoy either at home or afield. It also enables you to satisfy the ethical obligation to use every possible part of the animal.

Proper field care requires extra effort when you're looking forward to this traditional deer-camp feast. The tenderloins, of course, aren't going anywhere until you remove them, but the liver and heart demand some extra attention; your field-dressing technique may need some work. While some deer hunters easily roll out the entrails in a neat package, some of the piles I have come across appear as if the hunter went to work with an ax instead of a knife. once you remove the entrails, detach the heart and liver immediately and set them aside to cool before placing them in a plastic bag.

Of the three meats which compose our opening day feast, the tenderloins are the most familiar. For hunters accustomed to taking the whole animal to a processor, look inside the cavity after hanging the deer. The tenderloins will be the two "snakes" on either side of the backbone. You can feel them as separate muscles, and they are easily removed with a sharp knife and some judicious feeling around.

Probably the most common way of preparing tenderloins is to cut them into three- or four-inch-long segments. Then make a slit across, cutting almost all the way through each section. Fold the section in half and broil it like a beef steak. The problem here is that tenderloin, a very lean meat even on domestic cattle, is even leaner when it's called venison. Broiling can produce dried out, stringy results rather than what should be the best meal you eat this year.

Using a mildly-flavored marinade which enhances, but doesn't overpower the natural flavor of the tenderloin, and gently frying it in butter overcomes the dryness and offers an easy, no-hassle alternative to the broiler grate.

Marinated Camp Venison Tenderloin
Venison tenderloin, sliced 1/2 to 3/4 inch thick
Butter or oil for frying
2 cups olive oil
1 cup red wine
2 bay leaves
1/2 sliced onion
1 teaspoon garlic powder or 1 garlic clove
Sprinkling of black pepper
Mix the olive oil, wine, and spices, and marinate the meat overnight. Fry the venison slices slowly in the butter or oil over moderate heat in a steel or cast iron pan.

Hunters turned off at the mention of a marinade are probably the victim of one of the bitter, vinegar-based concoctions found in many game recipes. I've converted more than one broiled-deer-tenderloin lover with this recipe, and you will too.

Deer Liver—A Succulent Treat

Feelings about liver seem to run to either love or hate, with no middle ground allowed. Like you, my mother force-fed me liver because "It's good for you," and perhaps, like me, you never recovered from the experience and grew up regarding liver as a great cat food ingredient but something definitely not suitable for human consumption.

For you liver-haters out there, just take my word for it--deer is different. Those vile, evil-looking brown slices accompanied by a baleful motherly glare have as much relation to fresh, pan-fried venison liver and onions bubbling in butter as the previously mentioned cat food does to a steak dinner.

Deer liver, heart, and a few fresh vegetables—the makings of a memorable deer camp feast.

Getting a liver back to camp doesn't guarantee good eating, however. It needs to be sliced thin—the thinner the better—then dipped in flour that has been seasoned with salt and pepper and cooked slowly and carefully. This is one dish you can't put on the heat and forget while you get the rest of the meal going. If you use too much heat you're back to square one, gnawing on a shoe sole and reliving those childhood memories. When done, your liver slices will be firm to the touch, like pressing your finger lightly against the underside of your forearm. Get them out of the pan without delay and you'll have no complaints and a lot of talk about how they just can't believe this is liver. My deer camp currently includes four others who have also cooked professionally at one time or another and one fourteen-year-old, and the consensus is that livers will no longer be left in the we

Pan-fried Venison Liver
Fresh venison liver, sliced no thinner than 1/4 inch
1 onion, sliced thin
2 cups flour
2 teaspoons black pepper
2 teaspoons salt
Butter or cooking oil for frying
Add the salt and pepper to the flour, mix, and coat the liver slices with the seasoned flour. Fry the onion in the butter or oil first, followed by the liver.

Try the Heart Too

We find food prejudices in every culture. The deer hunter chuckling at a Hindu for not eating beef will likely turn up his nose at the thought of eating heart, and this while eating a plate of over-easy chicken embryos and washing that down with an excretion from a cow.

Ancient hunters believed that eating the heart of your quarry endowed you with some of the attributes of that animal. While there isn't much in the way of scientific evidence for that theory, it's like a traditional cold remedy—while it might not help, it certainly can't hurt. I don't know about you, but my woodsmanship can use all the help it can get.

One way of introducing different foods to the leery is by camou-
flaging it the first time. I've seen crayfish served as shrimp and Rocky
Mountain oysters passed off as fried clams. Cold, sliced heart served
in a sandwich is one way of getting your foot in the finicky eater's door.

Most outdoor cookbooks contain a recipe for stuffed heart on the
last page, right by the porcupine chowder and armadillo stew. The
recipes require an oven and time, items often found singly in deer
camps but seldom together.

Braised deer heart takes less than an hour to prepare, from start to
finish. It's made on a stove top or over an open fire in one skillet, and
it's guaranteed to be the high point of the season if the cook does his
or her part.

The heart will be contained in a membrane when you remove it
from the animal. Leave this on while carrying the heart back

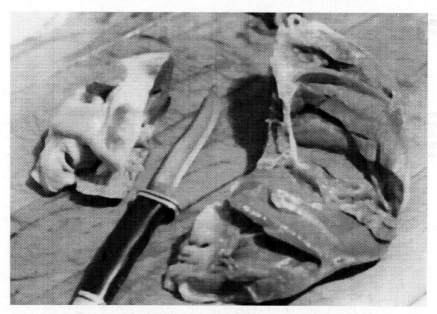

*Remove the entire top of the heart, and cut down
one side and open like a book.*

to camp to keep it clean. To prepare the heart for cooking, remove
the membrane and any fat, cut off the top which contains most of
the blood vessels and valves, then cut down one side and unfold it

like opening a book. Trim any membranes and blood vessels from the meat, and cut it into strips the size of your little finger.

Braised Deer Heart

One heart, cleaned and cut in strips 1 cup red wine
One onion, diced
Several bouillon cubes or beef gravy mix oil for frying
One small can of mushrooms (or better yet, some
    that you have picked from around camp)
The seasoned flour from the liver
A couple of vegetables like carrots, green peppers,
    celery, etc.
1/4 teaspoon garlic powder
1/4 teaspoon black pepper

Dip the strips of heart meat in the seasoned flour you made for the liver, brown it in the oil, and when its cooked half through add the onions, carrots, or whatever vegetables are handy, the mushrooms, a bouillon cube, and a shot or two of red wine, and then cover it tightly.

Cook it until the vegetables are done. The whole business will thicken up a bit and can be set aside in a warm place while you prepare the liver or tenderloins. Some noodles are nice with this.

For the camouflaged heart sandwiches mentioned earlier, try this:

Deer Heart Sandwich Meat

One deer heart, trimmed and cleaned
1 teaspoon black pepper
1 teaspoon salt
4 bay leaves
2 cloves garlic
1 tablespoon Worcestershire Sauce

Boil the heart in enough water to cover it and the other ingredients. Continue until it's cooked through, then give it another half hour. A pressure cooker works even better. Cool it in the refrigerator overnight and slice it thin for sandwiches.

If this trick doesn't fly, at least save your heart to grind with your burger or sausage meat.

Braised deer heart is simple to prepare and guaranteed to be one of the high points of the season if the cook does his part.

Making Jerky

What about all the rest of that deer meat? Butchering deserves an entire book, and there are several fine ones on the market. Cooking venison in camp is treated in the different chapters in this book which deal with cooking techniques. We are talking about some basic camp cooking here, however, and probably the most basic camp and trail food of all is—jerky.

Jerky is any lean, red meat which has been lightly cured with a solution of salt and spices and then dried, either mechanically or naturally. The typical routine for pre-industrial hunters, whether of this age or in times past, was to gorge themselves with fresh meat at the place of the kill and dry the rest over slow, smoky fires. The drying process not only preserves meat by removing much of the water content (therefore making it unpalatable to bacteria); it also reduces the weight substantially. A pound of fresh meat ends up as about four ounces of jerky.

Jerky is dried—not cooked—meat. Simply and basically, one only has to apply slow heat, on the order of 100 to 125 degrees Fahrenheit, until the meat is dry. This process is made easier and tastier, however, by applying some sort of a salt cure beforehand.

Jerky can be made in camp, of course, but there's no reason to do so outside of a survival situation. Make your jerky at home, where the process can be done efficiently and almost effortlessly, and use the finished product for trail meals, snacks, or lunches while in camp.

To make jerky, take any lean meat, wild or tame, and cut into 1/8 to 1/4-inch-wide strips, cutting against the grain if possible. Cutting with the grain will result in a little chewier product, but is not a big problem if the structure of the chunk of meat you're cutting makes it expedient to cut it that way. Trim every piece of fat you possibly can from the meat. Remember, you are drying, not cooking the meat, and fat left in quantity will turn rancid.

The next step is the salt cure. The simplest way is just to use a strong solution of salt and water. This can be improved with the addition of various spices, as you will see in the jerky recipe in this chapter. Leave the meat in the cure overnight under refrigeration. The salt will draw the juices, blood, and some of the moisture from the meat strips, replacing them with salt and spices.

Finally, apply the heat. If you are making jerky in camp, you will have to construct or jury-rig some sort of frame to hold the meat away from the fire and to keep insects at bay and yet allow smoke to surround it. The fire must be tended constantly, and if you cover the fire with a canvas, for instance, you must be aware of the fire danger. Fine results in camp can be had by using the Coleman camp stove on top of a gasoline oven, but again, why? The price of fuel

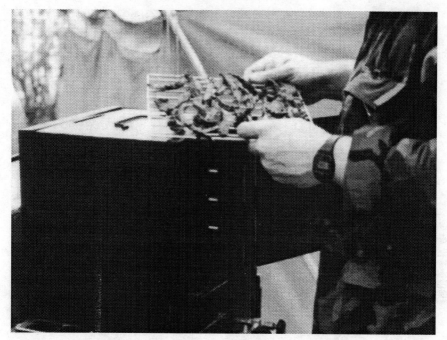

While jerky can be made in camp, it is easier to
dry it at home and carry it for lunches and snacks.
This batch is coming out of a Coleman camp oven.

to run the stove that long is prohibitive, you have to stay in camp to supervise the drying process because you can't leave a burning stove unattended for safety reasons, and the small capacity of the stove precludes drying any respectable quantity of meat. Outdoor jerky making in the humid months in the southeastern United States and parts of the midwest is a real chore. It can be done, but the effort required taxes the patience to a degree guaranteed to drive almost anyone inside the house to the kitchen oven.

Making jerky at home is much simpler. Cut sections of fence or window screen to cover your oven racks. This will prevent the strips of meat from falling through, and save you the trouble of piercing each piece with a toothpick and hanging it from the racks in this manner as is recommended in many jerky recipes. Set an electric oven on its lowest setting, and check this with a thermometer. You may have to prop the oven door open a crack to maintain the 1 00 to 125 degree temperature range. Gas ovens usually work well with just the heat of the pilot light and shutting the oven door. But once again, check the temperature with a thermometer as all ovens are different.

Overnight will probably be enough time to finish your jerky, but this depends on the humidity, oven temperature, thickness of the slices of meat, strength of the salt cure, and just the general cussedness of cooking in which nothing ever works just the way a recipe says it will. Your jerky should be hard to bend with the fingers but not brittle to the point that it will snap in half. The strips will be dark, wooden-looking objects that don't look a thing like something good to eat, but the looks are definitely deceiving. A bowl left on the counter in my house will be eaten like popcorn by the kids, and it's just as popular in camp when it's time to throw together a lunch before heading out in the morning or for munching while dinner is cooking.

For a really simple jerky, perhaps the first batch you make, just use Worcestershire Sauce for your salt cure. Soak the meat overnight in enough Worcestershire to cover it, and then dry the strips in the oven. That's it, and the results are just as good as any more complicated recipe.

For something a little fancier, try this one. Liquid smoke is just that—the distilled essence of wood ashes or smoke. It is available in many grocery stores, though you may have to ask to find where they are stocking it.

Camp Jerky
Venison or other lean meat, cut in strips
1 cup red wine
1 cup water
1 cup Worcestershire Sauce
2 tablespoons garlic powder, or 1 garlic clove
1 onion, sliced
3 tablespoons liquid smoke
Mix the above ingredients, and soak the meat overnight. Dry the strips in the oven until they're hard, but not brittle.

Making jerky provides a great opportunity to experiment with new recipes. The salt and spice mixture in the above recipe can be replaced with any of the steak sauces (some of the thicker ones will have to be watered down) found in the grocery store, teriyaki sauces from the same source, wines, and any herb or spice from your spice cabinet that sounds like it would go well with meat. Chili powder or ground cumin works very well if you can stand the heat.

Cooking Small Non-game Animals

Judging from the comments of some outdoorsmen I have spoken to, one of the problems with utilizing some of the non-game animals (and even the common small game animals such as rabbits and squir-rels in camp) is that in opening the standard "outdoor" cookbook, the camp chef is presented with a really bewildering

The combination of some cooking know-how and small game, makes for some memorable camp feasts.

and complicated array of recipes. The problem, in a way, is like the camper that purchases one of the many fine edible wild plant field guides on the market. While these books on the whole are well written and illustrated, there is just too much to absorb at one time. (Skin the possum, parboil this animal, use this other one in a stew, soak this one in salt water overnight, cook this other one in a pressure cooker and then broil it, and so on until you just ice the animal and deal with it later at home.)

While I would be the last to suggest that you pass up classical American country dishes like possum with sweet potatoes or roast coon, introducing oneself to wild camp cooking calls, at least for starters, for some uncomplicated cooking methods. Let's look at a "universal" small animal cooking method that can be easily applied to any four-legged beast that's slated to appear on the camp menu. Leave the more complicated recipes, for the time being, in the realm of the home kitchen.

We've looked at proper field care, and let's remember that this is the first, and most important, step towards making a quality woods meal. The scent glands, if any, have been removed at the time of skinning. Trim all fat possible from the carcass. While fat makes up a considerable amount of the taste appeal of domestic beef or pork, game fat has a strong flavor that usually does not travel well with civilized tastes.

Depending on the size of the animal, either cut it in quarters or split the carcass up the front of the rib cage and make sure the pelvis is broken in front so the animal can lay flat on a broiler grate.

The carcass is going to end up on the broiler grate, over the campfire, but before we get to that final step it should be either soaked in salt water or parboiled. This step serves both to remove some of the blood and strong flavors from the meat, and in the case of parboiling, somewhat tenderizes it.

Parboil or soak? Figure that young or small animals will be more tender. Soak these in salt water anywhere from a few hours to overnight. older, larger animals will be tougher, as a rule. Boil the meat in very lightly salted water until it's done, but not to the point of its falling off the bones. Dispose of the water away from camp as you would garbage or dishwater since it will contain a layer of fat that may attract unwelcome camp visitors. The closer you get to bear country, the more this last bit of advice makes sense.

After it's been soaked or boiled, the meat is rinsed, salted and peppered, and placed on the grill. You'll need a slower fire, of course, for the soaked, uncooked meat. Baste it with the barbecue sauce of your choice as you go along, either a bottled variety or the recipe given later in this book.

Nothing to it. Take a skinned animal with the fat trimmed, and soak or parboil it. Then rinse, salt and pepper, and flop him on the grill with some barbecue sauce. As I mentioned earlier, this is close to the ultimate in simple outdoor cooking, but that fact certainly won't detract from the way it tastes. Don't forego any of the more complicated methods of preparation to remain strictly with this one, but "barbecued animal" doesn't take a back seat to any other camp dish, and it's the perfect first lesson in fireside wild meat cookery.

Birds can be handled in camp in almost the same manner. Dress and pluck or skin them, but never mind the soaking or parboiling. Split the birds up the front, through the breastbone, lay them front down on a flat surface, and flatten them out with the heel of your hand so that they lay nicely. Then lightly salt and pepper them, and broil them on the grate.

2

Shore Lunch

The wind in the morning blew strong and steady off the big lake. There were smells of fish and wet, cold, sand. The sunrise was red and gold against the choppy gray metal of the horizon. Rubber boots were crunching on wet sand, and low voices were talking of minnows and trout and weather. The surf pounded so loudly you had to shout to be heard.

It was a good-sized trout, respectable. He'd go thirty inches easy. The fish was pulled out of the Lake Michigan surf just after first light. He had that gleam of big water on him, the iridescent rainbow shine of flank and glowing steel of snout. His colors faded as he flopped in the sand. The other fishermen on the beach worked with their gear, baiting, casting, waiting. I had that evening's supper laying on the shore.

That trout looked pretty good later on, too, covered with butter and lemon juice and wearing crosshatched marks from the grill. The meat was snapping and popping and steaming over the fire, flanked by a pan of potatoes and onions and a battered, blackened cook pot of blood-red spiced wine. We were camped in a state forest for a weekend of late-winter Lake Michigan trout fishing. The canned ham that accompanied us was never opened. We ate fish.

Eating Off the Water

Eating off the land sometimes can be accomplished best by eating off the water. Pound for pound, this is where the bounty of the earth

*Though the traditional shore lunch calls for an open fire,
the gasoline camp stove will serve in areas
where fires are impractical or not permitted.
(Photo courtesy of the Coleman Company.)*

is—the oceans, lakes, rivers, streams, and ponds of the planet do a more efficient job of growing meat than the surface world.

Anthropologists note that the American Indian, as was common in a pre-industrial economy, devoted the majority of his time to securing enough food to meet his immediate needs. Though familiar outdoor foods like jerky and pemmican attest to the fact that surplus food was stored for winter seasons or other periods of food scarcity, the normal scheme of things demanded that the bulk of an Indian family's time was spent accumulating enough to eat for that day; they would deal with tomorrow when it came.

Unless fish figured into their economy. The Nootka Indians of the northwest United States were an example. Fishing the annual salmon run provided such an immense quantity of food that permanent wooden buildings of some accomplishment were constructed. The surplus was smoked, and a lively trade was conducted with neighbors. A more sophisticated economy was generated.

The benefits of a fish diet also manifest themselves in the animal kingdom. The grizzly bear runs about the same size wherever found until you hit the subspecies native to Kodiak, Alaska, and the other brown bears of that state. A diet of fish allows them to reach a monstrous size never attained by their cousins to the south who must grub about on land to make a living.

The only form of "market hunting" yet legal, and ethically acceptable, is commercial fishing. Though the domestic raising of fish on farms grows larger each year, the harvesting of wild fish looks like it will be with us for some time.

Batter-fried Fish Fillets

A northern pike that I took a few years back could have been the biggest one I have ever caught. It never did get measured or weighed properly, as we were four portages past the last road up in the Boundary Waters Canoe Area of northern Minnesota. It was about forty inches anyway—no trophy by most standards—but it sure made me happy.

We ate him for lunch, burning driftwood in a fire pit made of a hole scooped in the sand, the metal grate straddling two rows of rocks running along either side of the pit. I had gutted the fish and cut steaks crosswise, drizzled them with butter and lemon juice from my shore-lunch-making kit, and added salt and a little pepper. A can of beans, saved for the occasion, was bubbling in a pot to one side of the fire. With the sun shining and a light breeze, I was as close to paradise as I've ever been.

Anywhere in the northern part of the country, the shore lunch is a tradition of the north woods, made legendary by the old-time fishing guides of the big musky and walleye country of northern Minnesota, Wisconsin, Michigan, and Canada. They were as handy with the frying pan and fillet knife as with rod and reel and advice on where the fish will be today. The shore lunch became legendary in its own right. City dwellers up for fishing, realizing the memories of that day, often centered their activities around the midday meal.

The traditional shore lunch is fillets, fresh from the water, dipped in an egg and milk wash, breaded in a cornmeal or bread or cracker crumb mixture with a blend of seasonings known only to the guide or the guide's wife. A recipe for fish fillets cooked this way would be identical to the fried turtle recorded later in this chapter. Another favorite shore lunch that puts the frying pan to work is batter-fried fish. This one works great with rough or game fish alike.

Batter-fried Shore Lunch
Fish fillets, steaks, or chunks
Enough cooking oil to cover fish while cooking
2 cups Bisquick or bannock mix (from baking chapter)
2 cups milk (or use 1 cup milk and 1 cup beer)
2 eggs
1 teaspoon pepper
1 teaspoon salt

Heat the oil to almost smoking in a Dutch oven or wok. Mix the flour, salt, and pepper and set aside. Beat the eggs and mix them with milk or beer. Add Bisquick or bannock mix and stir to the consistency of pancake mix. First dust the fish in seasoned flour, then dip them in batter and add them directly to the hot oil. Fillets will float when done.

*If luck holds out, you can feed your camp with fish
without harming the resource.*

Don't Forget the "Non-game" Fish

It's possible to eat lots of fish in camp. Unless you are a professional fisherman, however, and can keep the larder filled with walleye pike and large-mouth bass fillets, you will likely have to overcome the stigma of eating only what local custom may define as "game fish," and avoiding those classified as "trash" or "rough" fish.

What constitutes good food is defined by local custom. The prime beef steak you enjoy today would gag a Hindu native of India, and doubtless likewise the plate of fried grasshoppers scarfed down by a North African tribesman would similarly affect you. Both are good food.

Let's note at this point that when I talk about "fish" I am using the term to include more than animals with fins and scales. We will discuss, with the idea of adding to the menu, other denizens of the deep, some with legs, some with claws, and so on. Come supper time, it's all fish to me.

A few of the species sometimes passed over by the game fisherman, usually for no other reason than food prejudice, are the carp, originally imported into this country from Europe as food fish; the freshwater drum, or sheepshead; the burbot, a close relative of the cod; the bullhead; catfish (that's right, some northerners would as likely eat a cat); crayfish; turtles; frogs; buffalo fish; gars; and suckers.

Besides the hook and line, many states allow rough fish and some other species to be taken by archery, spearing, traps, and setlines or trotlines. This book deals with cooking, not the taking of wild foods, but much of what we are doing here is looking at foods that we can utilize incidentally. By heredity we are dinner-table opportunists. Agriculture is only ten thousand or so years old and before that, stretching far back into the dim memories of prehistory, men ate what they happened across in the course of a day's hunting and gathering. We can do the same.

Carp, buffalo, bowfin, sheepshead, suckers, and some other species are often taken incidentally to the game fish species being sought. Others, such as turtles or frogs, usually have to be specifically pursued by other means than the standard hook and line. Dividing our newly-found selection of seafood into two groups labeled fish (fins), and non-fish (all the rest), let's start with fish.

Caring for Fish in the Field

In the field, care of fish is pretty simple. Gut the fish immediately, wash off the blood, and keep it cool. The vast majority of walleyes, northern pike, catfish, and other game fish that are taken on fishing and camping trips end up in the frying pan that same evening, as they should. Not only is it hard to transport fish during the warmer months of the year, but where is a better place to eat wild food than in camp?

There are many fish that are not eaten in camp, however, out of a mistaken notion that they're not edible. The carp, which is farmed in China, praised as a game fish in England, featured as a classic dish in the cuisines of Slavic countries, and which was introduced into the United States from Europe in the 1800s as a food fish by hungry Germans, is the best-known victim of this fallacy. The folks that go for fish fries in the taverns along the Mississippi and Illinois Rivers in southern Illinois enjoy fried carp, in sandwiches.

Need some more convincing? The Larousse Gastronomique, the comprehensive encyclopedia of classical French cuisine, lists nineteen recipes for carp. Fear not, we're not going to create a carp a la juive a l'orientale over a Coleman stove as the tent flaps in the breeze and the sun sets over the lake, I'm just demonstrating that eating carp isn't just a good idea that I dreamed up last week—this is an old food for us, and a good one.

After eviscerating the carp you should decide what you're going to do with him before you go any farther. Baked, stuffed fish, cooked in a reflector oven or whole on a grate, as we'll discuss further in this book, is best served by "fleecing" the fish. Starting at the tail with a fillet knife, work your way up the fish, removing strips of scales as you go. The skin is left intact. This procedure is also used if you'll be pickling or canning your catch.

Filleting a carp, buffalo fish, or sucker is no different than any other fish. Once the fillet is removed from the fish and skinned, however, another step may be taken. These fish, like the northern pike, have a row of Y-shaped bones running through the fillets. Cut a series of shallow slices with your fillet knife perpendicular to the length of the fillet, every 1/2 inch or so. This will allow the heat from cooking to soften the Y bones to the extent that you usually won't know they are there.

An occasional complaint about carp is of a musty or muddy flavor, usually in regard to fish caught in mid-summer. Remove the dark red flesh and "mud vein" that runs lengthwise along the fillet before scoring it and you will have solved this problem.

The buffalo fish is a member of the sucker family. An important member of the commercial catch, his fillets contain the Y bones of the carp and should be handled in the same manner.

The freshwater drum, or sheepshead, is common in fishing waters across the United States. Another victim of food prejudice, in one region the sheepshead will be tossed up on the bank and left to rot as a trash fish, while several hundred miles away anglers will specifically pursue him. The fillets contain no Y bones, and he makes a particularly fine pan-fried dinner.

The burbot is the only freshwater member of the cod family, and in the frying pan he is just as good to eat as his salt-water relative. Another fish that is reviled in one area and praised in another, clean the burbot like any other fish. There are no Y bones, and the fillets are excellent fried or broiled.

The point here is when in doubt, eat it. You have nothing to fear from fresh-water fish (with the possible exception of man-made pollution) other than perhaps running into something that is less than pleasing on the plate. The bowfin, or dogfish, for instance, has such soft, mushy flesh that cutting a fillet from it is like cutting cottage cheese—the consistency is about the same. If you freeze the meat for a month and then pickle it, it gains enough form to be eaten, though that's a lot of work for little return.

Pickled Fish

One method for utilizing rough fish resembles the way we use some of our venison as jerky—pickled fish. Do the work at home and enjoy the fish in camp.

Pickled Fish
6 cups white vinegar
4 cups sugar
2 cups water
1 tablespoon salt
1 large onion, sliced
3 tablespoons pickling spice

Boil the ingredients for 10 minutes to dissolve the sugar and spices. Reduce the heat, add chunks of fish, and simmer until the fish is just cooked through. Pack it in glass jars, insuring that the fish is covered with pickling liquid, and refrigerate. Let it stand for 5 days before eating.

Crayfish—A Southern Delicacy

If you had to pick one item that is close to universal in waters around the United States, easy to catch, and appeals to almost everyone's taste, it would have to be the crayfish.

If I told you about a lobster dinner I enjoyed with a friend, camped on a one-acre island shaded by a few of the last virgin pines left in this part of the country, surrounded by one of those jewels of cool, sky-blue northern lakes, you may ask why I mention such gourmet fripperies in a book dealing with eating off the outdoors. Lobster? What next, you sneer? Frozen lasagna?

The lobster we enjoyed was a native of the region, hauled kicking, dripping, and hopping mad from the shallows in front of our campsite in two wire traps. The crayfish, crawfish, crawdad, or mud bug, if you're from the South, is a close relative to his high-priced cousin, the lobster. So close, in fact, that if not for the diminished size you really couldn't tell the difference in the meat.

The first time I sampled crayfish was by treachery and subterfuge, though I would have voluntarily tried them if given the chance. One of those practicing sadists, of whom we all are acquainted with at least one, was a bartender in a restaurant where I was employed. Passing through the kitchen one afternoon with a tray of "shrimp cocktail"— little toothpicks, shrimp sauce, crushed ice, the works—he offered samples to the staff as he passed. "Thanks," we said. "They're crayfish," he replied. He didn't get the reaction that the chef in another place I worked did when he passed around the thin sliced, breaded and fried bull testicles which he claimed were fried clam strips, but he got his laugh out of it.

What I gained was an appreciation of one of the real treats of eating outdoors—a treat revered in the South almost as much as red beans and rice. How sad that in much of the country the crayfish is regarded as some kind of glorified aquatic insect which is good for bass bait, "but you'll never catch me eating one."

Accumulating enough crayfish for an appetizer or meal demands little in the way of labor. The most common methods are to turn over rocks in stream beds or lake shallows and scoop the little scudders up. You can dangle a piece of string or fishing line with a chunk of liver or similar aromatic meat attached over one and he'll grab a hold. A crayfish doesn't know when to let go, and you can swing him out of the water before he realizes that he is part of your meal planning for that day.

The fresh water lobster is easy to catch, simple to cook in camp, equal on a dinner plate to his salt-water cousin. (Photo courtesy of E.P. Haddon, U.S. Fish and Wildlife Service.)

These methods while entertaining, sporting, and educational, leave a lot to be desired if you actually wish to dine on the local lobsters. Minnow traps or seines, smelt seines, or a dip seine made specifically for crayfish work fine, or you can get serious. Crayfish trappers that trap for seafood wholesalers and retailers and biological supply houses use inexpensive homemade wire traps. While perhaps using

the trap will take all the sport out of actually going in after the little dev-
ils in a more active manner, they leave you with extra time so you can
spend your day fishing, hunting, taking pictures, hiking, laying on your
back watching the shapes of clouds cruising over the tops of pine
trees, or whatever else you choose, and when you head back in for the
day the work is done.

The crayfish trapper's trap is made by taking a 30-inch length of
1/2-inch or 3/4-inch mesh fencing of the standard width from the
hardware store, rolling it into a tube, and securing the sides with
wire. Close one end with wire except for a 1 1/2-inch hole in each
corner. Stand the trap up, with the open end down, and force the two
holes inside out with a quart pop bottle or similar object by pushing
down into the trap from the outside. You should end up with a pillow-
shaped tube of wire with two cones extending into the trap in one
end, and the other end open. To close the open end, just fold it over
and crease it.

*About the only way to gather enough crayfish for a serious
feed is to build a simple, inexpensive trap.*

Bait the trap with fish heads or just about any other meat-scraps type of material. Fasten the trap with a wire or rope, throwing it in water from three to twelve feet deep. Rocky bottoms make the best crayfish habitat, but I have taken full traps from sandy bottoms also.

Crayfish cooking is tailor-made for camp—it's simple and social and quick. Place the crustaceans in a container of clean water

*The professional trapper's crayfish trap is
simple, inexpensive, and efficient.*

to purge them of wastes and to clean off some of the grit. Overnight is great, but a few hours will do. You'll need a pot of boiling water large enough to hold the crayfish.

The Swedish recipe is the simplest.

Swedish Style Crayfish

Crayfish
Boiling salted water—enough to cover
A few sprigs of fresh dill or 1 tablespoon dried
    dillweed per dozen crayfish
    Plunge the live crayfish into the rapidly boiling
water. When the shells turn red they are done. Serve
with melted butter and lemon.

But I like the Louisiana crab boil style better.

Louisiana Style Crayfish

Crayfish
Boiling salted water—enough to cover
1 heaping tablespoon of crab boil or shrimp boil spice
    for each gallon of water
1 quartered lemon for each gallon of water
1 quartered onion for each gallon of water
    Boil the water, spices, and lemons and onions for
fifteen minutes. Add the crayfish, and remove them
when the shells turn red.

Cooking some potatoes or sweet corn in the crayfish pot before the
little lobsters go in makes a fine, easy one-pot meal.
    If you can't locate crab or shrimp boil spice in your (obviously north-
ern or western United States) grocery store, make your own.

Crayfish Boil Spice

1 tablespoon ground mustard seed
1 tablespoon cayenne pepper
1 tablespoon black pepper
1 teaspoon powdered bay leaf
1 teaspoon allspice
1/2 teaspoon powdered cloves
    One of the "Cajun"-style meat and seafood
seasonings found in the grocery store spice rack
will also work well.

Crayfish eating is as simple, natural, and fun as the catching and cooking. Shovel your feast out on a plate, flat rock, canoe bottom, or whatever eating surface your outdoor fine dining establishment provides. Seize a crustacean and twist off the tail. The "mud vein," or intestinal tract, will stay with the body, leaving you to pry the shell segments from the tail and eat. If you are fortunate enough to live in an area supporting one of the larger species of crayfish, up to six inches or so, the claw meat is worth pursuing. If you have a slow day in the crayfish trap and are left with a few animals but not enough for a meal, cook and freeze them at home, saving the tail meat for use in other recipes such as the fish stuffing mentioned in the over the Fire chapter.

I'm spending a lot of time here on one species of outdoor food to the exclusion of others, but crayfish deserve it. They are easy and inexpensive to trap, can be left in the trap indefinitely until needed, need no field dressing or care other than a soak before cooking, and when it comes to their qualities at table, they rank with the finest of gourmet meals. A crayfish feast in camp is a great place for the novice camp chef to begin.

Before getting involved in trapping or otherwise taking crayfish or any other non-game species, check your state game laws. Licenses may or may not be required, or there may be size or number restrictions placed on traps. Some species will be subject to closed seasons, and some are protected at all times.

Enjoying Turtle Meat

One way that some fur trappers and other rural people maintain their household cash flow during the summer months is by trapping turtles and selling the meat to fish wholesalers and restaurants. While the yards-long hoop-and-net turtle traps used by the pros are too much work for the recreational natural eater, taking turtles by unattended hook and line, where legal, is a productive method for adding another gourmet treat to the camp menu.

With sturdy hooks, a serious wire leader, and just about anything made of meat for bait, you're in business. Study the regulations in your state in regards to endangered species, and be sure to follow them. For eating purposes, however, all turtles taste about

Use a hefty treble hook and a wire leader for catching turtles.
Bait with any aromatic meat.

the same. The snapping turtle is the trophy, and with specimens ranging up to a foot long (measured across the shell) it is usually the turtle
that gets involved in dinner.

Snapping turtles have that name for a reason. Exercise care when
handling them. They are very aggressive and can move much quicker
than you would expect a turtle to move, coming almost off the ground
when they strike. Start preparing your turtle dinner by encouraging him
to bite a stick. Then while holding the stick away from the body to
stretch the neck, have a companion with a good eye and stout arm lop
off the head with a hatchet. Hang the turtle by the tail to bleed it.

There are two ways of removing the edible meat from the turtle.
The first is to boil the entire animal, shell and all, and as it begins to
cook, remove it from the water, slip the skin from the meat, and separate the top and bottom halves of the shell. This procedure is time consuming and quite a hassle in camp.

A quicker way is to lay the turtle on its back, cut away the lower
shell, then remove the meat from the tail, legs, and neck, and extract
the tenderloin which is located by the backbone. You may have to
remove the backbone with a pry bar of some sort to get at them.

When you think of turtles, turtle soup comes to mind. If you want
to save some time dressing the turtle, just get the meat out of the
shell, bones and all. After the meat has boiled for a while, it is easy

to separate the bones and gristle and break the meat up into smaller pieces. Finish up your turtle soup like this:

Camp Turtle Soup

Turtle meat from one turtle
1 large onion
Diced carrots, celery, and potatoes—
    enough to fill pot
Either beef or chicken bouillon cubes
Black pepper
    Boil the turtle meat in the water with some of
the beef or chicken bouillon until the meat can
be removed from the bones. Do that, then add
vegetables and cook until just done. Season with
the pepper.

Turtle can also be breaded and pan fried just like fish fillets, but it needs a little precooking first.

Fried Turtle

1 turtle, cleaned and cut into large pieces
Flour seasoned with salt and pepper
Oil for frying
2 beaten eggs
2 pints milk
Dry bread crumbs or cracker meal
    Parboil the turtle meat, separate it from the bones,
and cut the meat into bite-sized pieces or larger. Coat
it with the seasoned flour, dip it into the eggs, and coat
it with the bread crumbs or cracker meal. Fry it in an
inch or more of hot cooking oil.

Frog Legs

I've never been able to get together enough frog legs for more than a small snack before supper. If you are blessed with a population of bullfrogs, go after them at night with a light and a frog spear. Sportsmen pursue them during the daylight hours with standard fishing tackle using a plain hook baited with a strip of bright red cloth. I can't understand why a frog would want to eat something like that, but then neither can I understand why a northern pike chases after a red-and-white-striped oval piece of metal with a prominent hook attached to one end. It really does work.

What do frog legs taste like? The standard answer to that question is "chicken." That's for people who don't really want to eat them. Actually, they taste like frogs.

Clean a frog by cutting off the feet, cutting off the legs at the hip joint, and then slipping off the skin with the fingers. Cook the frog legs like you would a fried turtle, except there is no need to parboil them. Frog legs make a good before-dinner appetizer.

Mussels Aren't Recommended

Anyone conscious of crayfish, frogs, turtles, and the various species of fish available to the larder of the camper can't help but notice the profusion of clams and snails in many of our waters. I have eaten freshwater snails, baked in garlic butter, and have sampled some of the large, bivalve clams native to my area. Neither made a favorable impression.

Mussels, due to their sedentary life-style and water-straining, bottom-feeding table manners, become receptacles for PCBs, pesticides, heavy metals, and other pollution. Eating mussels from non-polluted areas poses the possibility that you are dining on one of the two dozen federally-determined endangered species of mussel. Staff biologists and researchers from the Department of Natural Resources that I have spoken to and corresponded with are generally pretty negative on the subject of eating mussels for the reasons outlined above. I don't eat them anymore and don't recommend the practice.

3

Foraging and Gathering

Though we spent part of the opening chapter establishing that our bodies can fare well on a diet of red meat, the use of plants as food plays an important role in our eating habits. The normal human condition is to be omnivorous. Plant foods can supply a complete, healthy diet for humans, though a rather complicated regimen of amounts and varieties of foods is needed to match the complete nutrition available from meat. Wild edible plants are as good for you, compared to domestic cultivated plants, as wild meat is to the domestic. An advantage of wild plants is that in most cases they won't carry the herbicide and pesticide residue found in some grocery store produce. It is pretty much agreed that the healthiest diet for us is a combination of plant and animal foods, so let's look at the vegetarian side of camp cookery.

The first wild edible plant to appear on our camp menu was the green bloom spikes of cattails gathered from a roadside marsh on the way to camp in the national forest. They were boiled in a small amount of salted water and eaten like corn on the cob. They were a hit at mealtime, precipitating an enthusiastic reaction from the diners just like the first bannock we turned out of a frying pan. Since then we continue to enjoy cattails and try to add other wild edibles to our repertoire each year.

The trouble with many of the edible plant field guides on the market is that they do too good a job, or at least too thorough a job. There is so much material covered in one book that the novice wild eater can't get a grip on one solid base to start out with. To the majority of us non-farm raised folks, until we learn otherwise, the plant world is one vast, green expanse. With the exception of the blatantly obvious, like a dandelion in bloom or a scattering of acorns beneath an oak, plants are not seen as individual species, or individuals, but seem to get divided loosely into weeds, lawns, and trees. My point here is that you will need a field guide even to utilize the few common species of plants we will examine in this chapter. But if you will pick one or more of the plant foods discussed here you'll gain the confidence to explore further. There really are an incredible number of edible plants which exist all around you, whether you are at home or in camp.

Criteria for Selecting Edible Wild Plants

The criteria I used to select plants for this chapter were that they be easy to identify, have a wide range in the United States, be relatively easy and foolproof to work with and, last but not at all least, taste good. We are looking here for more than just edible plants, we want good table fare. Though a really comprehensive field guide may list hundreds of edible species, many of them, quite simply, taste terrible or are so much work to process that the calories expended outweigh the benefit gained.

Dandelions

As in almost every area of human activity in these turbid times, a plant gatherer must take pollution into account. As you gather dandelions, as we will shortly discuss, you may want to start out by gathering from your lawn at home. Take into consideration any fertilizer, herbicides, or insecticides which may have been sprayed there or which may have drifted over from the neighbor's yard. Some of these compounds do not just safely fade away after they have done their dirty work—they persist in the soil or plants. On the same track, avoid gathering plants within 50 feet of busy roadways due to the settling of lead from automobile exhaust gases.

The dandelion is probably the most recognized wild edible in North America and makes a good place for us to start. It's easy to identify positively, has no poisonous look-alikes, is easy to gather and prepare, and ranges throughout North America. As we mentioned above, if you want to work with dandelions at home before trying them out while camping, the lawn is but a few short steps away, and I have yet to see a community without these "weeds." You will find higher quality eating plants from along the edges of grown-up areas, however, where they are not being constantly cut back like they are on the lawn.

In the spring pick the small leaves, before the flowers appear. As in any edible plant, the younger and smaller the plant part the better eating it will be. These leaves are good eaten raw; chopped raw and added to soups, stews, or omelets; or cooked like greens.

A little more complicated cooked form of dandelion is to take the flowers, dip them in batter, and fry them in hot oil. An easy way to make batter in camp is to take your dry bannock mix, or Bisquick if you prefer, and thin it with milk or water and beer to make a batter the consistency of a thin paste. Then dip the flowers in the batter and fry them in enough hot oil to cover.

A coffee can be made from dandelions by digging and washing the roots in the fall and winter, baking them until dry and grinding them, and then brewing them as you would ground coffee. It does not contain caffeine.

Many books will instruct the reader to cook dandelion leaves or other wild leaves "like greens," which is a bit of a forgotten art in some places. Here is the technique.

Cooked Wild Greens
Tender, young leaves
Wash in cold water to remove grit
Boil briefly in as little salted, buttered water as possible

Steaming greens will deliver better results yet, and if you have some bacon grease saved, substitute that for the butter.

Blackberries

Another wild edible that should already be familiar to the camp cook is the blackberry, also known as the raspberry, red raspberry, and by other local names. I mention memorable meals from time to time in this book; the breakfast that springs to mind without any coaxing was bannock pancakes, thick with the blackberries that my partner picked while I was making coffee and stoking up the camp stove.

The blackberry grows on a thick, bristly, thorny bush, and in a good berry year will be covered with the fruits, red while immature and shiny black when ready to pick and eat. They range throughout the United States in the form of one similar species or another, with the berries ready to pick in midsummer. As jelly making is out of the picture for the camp cook, the only use for the blackberry is to be eaten as a raw fruit or as an addition to pancakes, muffins, or breads. That's enough, though.

You can brew a tea from the leaves, as you can from many edible plants, but it is such a poor second to the wintergreen tea that we'll look at a little later, and many other wild teas, that I don't personally feel it's worth the effort.

Cattails

The cattail takes the honors as the most versatile edible wild plant, offering some sort of nourishment in each season of the year. Identifying the cattail is easy. Nothing else looks quite like its brown, sausage-like flowers, though other species do closely resemble the green leaf structure of the cattail. Make sure there is a "cat tail" attached to the plant and you can't go wrong in the identification department.

The cattail ranges throughout the shallows, river bottoms, and wetlands of North America, and is such a tough and prolific plant that the wild diner normally need not worry about taking too much from any one area.

Starting in the early spring, the cattail offers its bloom spikes, the young, green spikes protruding from the top of the flower. Snip these off, leaving a piece of stem as a handle. Remove the papery

The cattail is one of the few wild edible plants that offers some type of food in all four seasons.

husks, then cook, season, and eat them just as you would corn on the cob, boiling them in salted water and serving with butter.

The tender shoots, known as "cossack asparagus," are found by separating the long, slender leaves down to the bottom of the plant and pulling out the white, tender shoots. These can be eaten raw or cooked like the spikes and used like asparagus. A plate of these dressed with the Hollandaise sauce from the Sauces chapter will provide a meal not soon forgotten.

Come summertime the bloom spikes you didn't eat will form coats of downy yellow pollen. Gather this by rubbing it loose from the stalks over a bag, and clean it by pressing it through a fine mesh which will break it up into the consistency of flour and separate out any foreign matter. Use your cattail pollen flour as a substitute for one half the flour in any pancake recipe, or simmer the pollen in water and eat it as a porridge, or use it as a thickener in soups or stews.

During the fall and winter months the cattail offers the little horn-shaped sprouts along the roots as a crunchy salad ingredient or snack. To pull up roots and trim the sprouts bring your shovel, since this is wet, muddy work. For the ambitious camp baker, the roots of the fall and winter cattail can provide a flour which can be substituted for half the wheat flour in any baking recipe. Pull up the plants and rinse them. Remove the outer skin of the roots while it's still fresh and flexible, and

Collect cattail roots in the fall and process them into flour.

soak the starchy root cores in water. The flour will settle on the bottom. Pour off as much water as possible, then repeat the process and allow the flour to dry.

Acorns

Some people are surprised when they are told that acorns are not only edible, but served as a major food source for Indians in the United States up until this century. In a way I can understand their feelings. Indeed, I wonder how man ever came to eat acorns, as the ones that I have tasted right from the tree have been very bitter from the tannic acid content. Some species of oak are found all throughout the United States and all are edible. The acorns will appear in the late summer and fall.

Though there are a few species that are mild-tasting enough to eat raw, most acorns must be treated before they can be considered edible by humans. The treatment is to first crack the shells. I use a wooden board and the driveway to crack mine and then I soak the acorns for a few hours, followed by changing the water and another soak, this time overnight. Try one. Depending on the tree, some acorns may taste good at this point while others will need another soak, and if that fails boil them in two changes of water. The tannic acid that causes the bitter taste is soluble in water, it just depends on how much of it your particular acorns hold.

Grind your shelled, leached acorns into flour. The easiest way is to use a blender. Shoot for the consistency of cornmeal or a little finer.

Don't wait too long to process your acorns. Worms will develop in some batches if they're not used. And if they're stored in an area accessible to rodents, you can wave them goodbye. I left several bushels in the garage and within a week they were gone, hauled off one by one, a winter cache for the resident mouse population.

Try making some bread with your acorn flour. This one is a baking powder bread so it can be made in camp in your Dutch oven or reflector oven without too much trouble.

Acorn Bread

1 cup acorn flour
1/2 cup cornmeal
1/2 cup whole wheat flour
1 tablespoon baking powder
4 tablespoons salad oil
1 teaspoon salt
1/4 cup honey
2 eggs
1 cup milk

Mix the dry ingredients. Mix and add the liquid ingredients, taking care not to over mix. Bake at 350° for twenty to thirty minutes, or at a moderate heat in the Dutch oven.

Another American Indian dish using the acorn is this stew.

Acorn Venison Stew

2 lbs or so of cut-up venison
1 cup fine ground acorn flour
Salt and pepper

Roast the meat in water until cooked through. Season it with salt and pepper, and add acorn flour to thicken it.

Wintergreen

Now that we have found something to eat, how about a cup of tea to wash it down. As I mentioned earlier, many of the herb teas from wild plants just don't cut it in the beverage department. This isn't just my opinion. In the wild edible plants courses I have taken through university extension divisions, we always seem to end up sampling a wide variety of teas at the end of one of the field trips. Everyone has different tastes, of course, but the only one sure hit is always a mint tea, and one of the most prolific and easily identified mints is wintergreen.

Wintergreen is a modest, unobtrusive, shy little plant, hugging the acid soils of evergreen forests throughout most of the United States.

The leaves are shiny and leathery, and the plant bears small, red berries in the fall and winter. Once you think you have spotted wintergreen pick a leaf, crush it with your fingers, and put your nose to work. The minty wintergreen smell is strong and unmistakeable.

The leaves of the wintergreen are usable in all seasons, and the berries are available in fall and winter. Make tea by using fresh leaves. This plant loses much of its potency when dried. Simply crush the leaves and pour on the hot water. The leaves are also good in salads, chopped in omelets, or anywhere else a mint taste is welcome. Chew the berries on the trail or add them to pancakes or bannock as you would blackberries.

Another use for wintergreen is as a marinade ingredient. Try this in camp with fresh-caught fish.

Wintergreen Fish Marinade

1 cup salad oil

6 tablespoons lemon juice

$1/2$ teaspoon tarragon

2 dozen wintergreen leaves, crushed

Mix all the ingredients. Marinade the fish for 24 hours. Make enough marinade to cover the fish, or to baste it several times. Bake or broil in a reflector oven or directly on a grate.

Sulphur Shelf Mushrooms

There is a joke that the bravest man in history was the guy that ate the first raw oyster. But since we are merely speculating here I would give my vote to the guy that ate the second mushroom, right after the guy who died from eating the first.

Any book or article on edible mushrooms contains warnings on the dangers of eating the wrong ones, as well they should. As one of my instructors liked to announce on the first day of each new class, "There are old mushroom hunters, and there are bold mushroom hunters. But there are no old and bold mushroom hunters." Eating wild mushrooms, if you know what you are doing, is certainly less dangerous that the drive in your automobile to the woods where you are picking them. The key is to be able to positively identify the different species. Unless you have a rural, old-country grandmother who can lead you through the complicated and confusing world of mushrooms where the common or slang name for a species may differ from region to region, or where some differing species share the same names, you are best off looking for a wild edible mushroom field trip. Inquire about them through your state university extension or museum.

A mushroom has about as much food value as a rock. If you ever find yourself foraging in a survival situation you would be best off ignoring this food source and finding one that has something to offer besides water, the primary ingredient of the mushroom, and a negligible amount of protein.

The sulphur shelf mushroom is one that you could use by identifying it only from a field guide. It looks like little else except perhaps another shelf mushroom, of which none are poisonous though most don't taste very good. To illustrate the mass confusion generated by using common names in this game, this species is also known as the chicken of the woods, or chicken mushroom. To confuse matters further, there is another species known as the hen of the woods. The scientific name of the sulphur shelf is Laetiporus sulphureus, or Polyporus sulphureus. Using one of those names will straighten things out if you look for this edible in a field guide.

The sulphur shelf is found attached to various species of trees, both conifers and hardwoods, throughout the United States. It is edible from May through November, depending of course on your particular area. Like any other plant, mushrooms lose their value as food as they get older, with shelf mushrooms gaining the succulent tenderness of a steel-belted tire as they reach the end of their lifespans. It is a common looking shelf-type mushroom like you see attached to many trees, except for its yellow-orange color and typically large size, growing up to thirty inches wide.

Use the outer parts of the sulphur shelf; avoid the core of the mushroom, the part which is attached to the tree, as it will be somewhat chewy. When you cut into this mushroom you will notice the grainy texture with a really phenomenal resemblance to cooked chicken breast. I would speculate this is the source of the mushroom's other name, chicken of the woods, because it tastes like a mushroom to me.

The sulphur shelf is easily identified, though a little effort may be required to collect a specimen.

The sulphur shelf mushroom is found attatched to trees throughout the United States.

Use the sulphur shelf in any dish just as you would use fresh mushrooms from the produce counter. Or, if you come across a particularly large specimen, large enough to slice like a pineapple, cook it like this.

Camp Poached Shelf Mushroom

Slices of sulphur shelf, 1/4 inch thick
Enough water in a frying pan to cover
one chicken bouillon cube
1 teaspoon tarragon leaves

Bring the water to a point just under a boil; do not allow it to boil. Add the tarragon leaves, crush the bouillon cube and add. Poach the slices until tender to a fork.

The sulphur shelf mushroom is a welcome and tasty wild addition to camp meals.

4

A Hearth Away
From Home

According to archaeological evidence, as long as 35,000 years ago man included a hearth, a place for the making and keeping of fire, in his shelters. Though the idea of cooking had yet to occur to anyone, the hearth served both to ward off the chill brought by cold winds blowing off mile-high glaciers and as the social gathering place it continues to be today in the form of fireplace, kitchen, and campfire.

As cooking caught on, practical camp cooking at this early date bore a close and remarkable resemblance to cooking at home. In both cases it involved the heave and scrape method in which an animal, or piece of an animal, was heaved into the fire and after roasting on a bed of coals was retrieved, some of the ashes and glowing embers scraped off, and after working through scales or hide it was dinner alfresco. Practical camp cooking hasn't changed that much in the last 35,000 years, I guess.

If you accuse me of using the word "hearth" loosely you are correct. As a place to cook and perhaps stay warm, a hearth can range from a fire pit with a supplementary two-burner gasoline stove and a cabinet full of utensils and food to feed a camp full of fishermen, hunters, or summer campers, to one end of a nylon backpacker's tent, the solitary occupant boiling water over a tiny mountaineers' stove in anticipation of a freeze-dried supper. The hearth is as essential to your camp as it is to your home and deserves a little more attention than it usually gets.

A hearth can be as simple as a backpacker's stove,
or elaborate enough to feed an entire camp.

The Stove vs. Open-fire Controversy

Let's begin with fire, the heart of the hearth. Entire chapters of books and countless hours of conversation and argument have been devoted to the ethical, ecological, and practical aspects of stoves versus wood fires. Without getting bogged down in any philosophical swamps, let's take a quick look at these arguments so that we can see where we stand. The stove-versus-campfire controversy is divided into the ethical, which some would call the ecological, argument, and the practical argument, which concentrates on which form of fire is of more practical use to the camp cook at a given time.

As the years in camp slip by, you'll find some of the fondest memories are centered around mealtime.

Memories of trips often revolve around meals and around the fire. They might focus on a roaring, snapping campfire warding off the chill in a snow-covered early-winter deer camp deep in a brooding northwoods forest, or they might recall a diminutive blaze of driftwood frying a trout, heating a can of beans, and warding off the foggy river chill on an early-spring evening. At any rate, hunkering down around a fire is one of the primitive urges which remains strong within us, defying the call of central heating and space heaters.

If you suspect at this point that I am a lighter of campfires you have guessed right. But before I am accused of ignoring any of the ecological arguments against fires let me qualify that. I totally agree that there are situations where fires are out of place. Heavily used campsites along backpacking or canoe trails, and situations in which a fire danger exists, are two examples. I have a problem with some of the arguments some folks raise against open campfires on an ethical" or "ecological" basis, though.

One of those arguments is that fire rings or pits are left uncovered at campsites and that these are unsightly and inconsiderate to the next party that may happen along. I agree with this point in most cases, but I also have a problem with cans, bottles, food scraps, and other litter. My point is that littering is not prevented in most cases by banning the litter, but rather by education, and to some extent, legislation. "Leave only footprints" is the current outdoor ethic and education the key, not the banning of one type of litter or of a certain activity, such as fire lighting, that may be the cause of a littering situation.

Another persistent argument is that burning itself is harmful. Current environmental science recognizes the importance of forest and prairie fires to the health of many plant and animal species. Fire, in itself, is not a harmful force but a natural and beneficial force of renewal. The proportionately tiny amount of wood consumed by the planet's campers will neither be missed because it has not decomposed directly into the soil nor will the smoke and ash produced be noticed, particularly among the spreading industrial pall belched daily from the urban centers of the world.

Overuse of some campsites can lead to all the available down and dead wood being used, and thoughtless overnighters starting

Situations where open fires are not allowed or are
impractical are served by the camp stove.
(Photo courtesy of the Coleman Co.)

in on the green wood. Perhaps, under these circumstances and in some of these places, campfires should be banned in favor of the stove.

I guess my main problem with the preceding arguments is that from an ecological point of view I would rather see us burn a renewable natural resource—trees—than the non-renewable gasoline, kerosene, or butane fossil fuels, some of which come packed in disposable, non-reusable containers.

Enough. Practically, from the standpoint of the physical demands of your camping trip and menu, the question of whether the stove should come along looks like this:

Campfire	Stove
Takes time you may not have to light.	Fast.
Use depends on weather.	Can be used in any weather.
No need to carry fuel.	No need to gather fuel or depend on finding it.
No weight or space requirements.	Must be carried.
One less machine to clean, fill, maintain, etc.	One more machine to clean, fill, maintain, etc.
Can be sat next to and enjoyed while listening to night sounds.	Not really suitable for sitting around.
Will dry wet clothing.	No way.

The above illustrates that while the campfire can provide you with many things denied the stove-only camper, the ideal is to use the wood fire for much of your camp cooking—and lazing around, while using the stove for rainy days, hot lunches on the trail, hot drinks and breakfast, and so forth. Whether a stove sees regular use or is tucked away in pack or vehicle for an emergency, every practical camp cook should own one.

The Heat-Fuel-Oxygen Triangle

Before looking into the building and use of campfires, let's look at what fire is. Fire is a chemical reaction, quite a violent one, in fact, once it gets going. Getting a fire started is sometimes a challenge. Think of fire as a triangle, with one leg being heat, the second fuel, and the third oxygen. As with a triangle, take away any of the legs and it ceases to exist. A fire is a tad more complicated than just putting those three factors together, of course, as they must exist in the proper quantities or intensities, but if you keep the triangle in mind on those wet, windy afternoons when it's your job to start the fire it will make that job a lot easier.

Campfire Safety

With the exception of the fair-sized blaze necessary to bake with a reflector oven, campfires for cooking are small fires. Small fires can be controlled. They don't sprinkle tents and sleeping bags with sparks. They allow you to keep warm, if the season calls for it, by staying close to the fire as opposed to staying out of range of the blasting heat of the novice's inferno special. And small fires use less fuel—fuel that you have to gather and cut.

When selecting the spot on which to build your fire, make safety the primary concern. Common sense rules here. Avoid overhanging branches, areas littered with pine needles, and, if possible, soils composed of largely organic material which could continue to smolder long after the campfire supposedly has been extinguished.

Safety with your fire isn't limited to getting it started and caring for it. While it's difficult to make a trip to the woods these days without hearing from several sources that fires should be drowned and stirred, many campers can tell horror stories, either from first-hand experience or from an acquaintance, of fires that had every appearance of being dead, but came back to life. To the "drown and stir" school of thought I would like to add "drown, stir, and dig." Tree roots are the usual offenders, smoldering underground until they work their way back to the surface, sometimes days later. This type of occurrence is both uncommon and difficult to imagine. But believe me, it happens.

The Basic Trench Fire-lay Design

A depressing aspect of fire building are those first attempts to do it "by the book." I mean the Boy Scout Field Manual, U.S. Air Force Survival Manual, and many of the fine publications that have drawings of fires that are architectural masterpieces of intricate design. They depict a perfectly straight and evenly trimmed log reflecting wall to the rear. Cook pots are shown suspended from a framework of sticks, with twig hooks holding the bails of the pots, a crosspiece holding the hooks, perfectly planted and trimmed upright sticks holding the crosspiece, and a stack of firewood organized and sorted by size and length. That's discouraging to the point of despair when compared to your own initial efforts, but campfires are just not like those pictures in real life.

One basic fire lay will serve the purpose of most any camping situation by increasing or decreasing its size as needed. Either dig a slit or trench, or build a similar arrangement with rocks. A combination of the two, a trench with a line of rocks along each lip, works best. A trench about twice as long as it is wide, from around two feet long and a foot wide for one or two campers or twice that size for a larger camp, will serve both the cooking needs of the camp and the warmth, or heating needs if demanded by the season.

As I mentioned above, if possible dig a trench. Line each side with rocks for the purpose of laying a grate across the trench for cooking. Avoid rocks which have been submerged in water or very moist soils. Trapped water within porous rocks can cause them to explode when heated. A shortage of rocks can be dealt with by digging the trench deeper or using a pair of green logs, which will eventually burn through. Absence of a trench, due to rocky ground, for instance, can be dealt with by building up the sides with rocks or a couple of green logs.

As we will see as we go along, this fire lay serves to bring plenty of oxygen to the fire through either end of the trench. It allows the efficient use of fuel, keeps the heat inside the fire and directly on the food, and provides an easy method of controlling the amount of heat bearing on each section of the grate.

For an example of how not to do it, let's take a trip into the national forest. Though I doubt that the United States Forest Service has a written policy regarding the banning of quality outdoor cooking in its campgrounds, it seems so from the types of fire enclosures they provide. Even in some of the backcountry canoe campsites they have built monstrosities of steel and concrete. Typically these are great circular orifices which rise a foot or more out of the ground. They defy any attempt to make a small fire and challenge the camp cook to produce an edible meal. The grate is too high off the ground and the inside capacity of the fire pit is too large. I do my best to avoid them.

The trench fire lay. Nearby leaves and grass, particularly in the fall, must be kept away from the flames.

The trench fire pit allows the camp cook to get a good, hot initial blaze underway. As the fire burns down into coals he can maintain a hot fire and keep it fueled at one end of the trench while cooking at the other end. The narrow width of the trench freely admits oxygen to the fire. The length of the trench allows a steady supply of fuel to be fed into the fire while keeping a supply of coals to cook over at the cooler end of the trench. As you can see, all three legs of the fire triangle are supported.

If there is a single, primary problem area with fires in the case of most campers I have observed, other than wet fuel, it is a lack of oxygen to the base of the fire. Without a constant stream of air when starting up the fire, your efforts are doomed. You are already dealing with a lack of heat because the trench is cold and probably somewhat damp and the fuel must be heated and dried before it will ignite. If one leg of the fire triangle is weak (in the above case heat), you have to strengthen another leg, oxygen.

Selecting Wood for Your Campfire

The drawings in the survival books of the perfect fire lays are often followed with a list of every known variety of wood found in North America, accompanied by a commentary on each fuels' suitability for burning. The idea is that the camp cook should sift through the down trees and brush in the area, sorting and squeezing as on a foray through a roadside fruit stand, and selecting only the finest of species for his cook fire—gourmet wood. While this is good knowledge to have, it's intimidating to the newcomer.

In my experience, and that of those more experienced than I from whom I have learned, there is one type of wood of interest to the camp cook and that is dry wood that is close to camp. Pine is often the best for starting a fire due to its flammable pitch content, but it will sometimes impart its flavor to the food. Hardwoods—maple, oak, hickory—burn into long-lasting, hot, fragrant coals that are a delight to cook over. If you have these woods close to your campsite, great. Burn them. If not, do not despair, the evergreens work fine when that is all you have.

Poisonous species shouldn't be burned in a campfire. Poison ivy and oak, for example, only become more so when burnt, the smoke from the flames carrying the irritants along with it.

If you can locate any apple and cherry trees, gather dead branches from them for the cook fire. The woodsy, aromatic flavoring these woods can add to foods won't work for a pot of oatmeal, of course, but a handful of apple or cherry wood tossed on the coals will add a delightful note to broiled meat, fish, or vegetables.

Stocking up a supply of wood can range from a single individual gathering an armload or two for an overnighter along a canoe trail to a crew of four or five with a chain saw and axes putting up a waist high stack of split logs for a week's stay in the woods over the deer season. Wood-gathering regulations range from disturbing nothing in some protected areas to cutting any dead or down wood you like, as in many national and state forests. Check before you cut. Look for dead logs leaning against other trees—those laying directly on the ground may be too wet to burn well.

When gathering tinder, take your time and gather only those sticks that are so dry they have taken on a grey or white color. Tinder that is the slightest bit green will often defeat even the best-laid plans for a fire. Some attention here will deliver more end results than any other aspect of putting together your fire lay.

Camp fire wood should start with twigs and graduate to larger chunks of wood as the fire grows in size.

Wood-Cutting Tools

Just because you are going to burn man's original campfire fuel doesn't mean you have to use the original cutting tool. The carbon steel, fiberglass-handled axes hanging in the hardware store these days may appear to be a far cry from the primitive stone ax with a wood handle, but not as far as you think. Writers have been down-playing the use of an ax in camp for a couple of decades now, and

Instead of using an ax, try a bow saw and perhaps a hatchet.

it seems to be finally catching on. The ax is a tool of massive distur-
bance in an era of "leave only footprints." It's a wilderness conquering
tool which sometimes is out of place at a time when we are trying to
conquer ourselves and leave the wild places alone.

Aside from aesthetic objections to the ax, it is just not the most
efficient tool for the job. With the exception of splitting wood that has
been cut with a saw, the saw is the tool of choice. From chain saws
in established camps that can be reached by truck or pack horse to
the canoe tripper's folding Swede saw, saws are proving to be of real
value to today's camper.

Saws for camp cooks include the triangular folding Swede saw,
the folding saws in which the blade slips into the handle like a great

jackknife, and the wire saws which are blades with rings for the fingers on either end. This last device should be perhaps saved for a survival kit rather than being considered basic equipment. Trying to saw through anything substantial with one of them resembles penance more than woodcutting.

Fire Starters

Heat, the final leg of our fire triangle, after oxygen and fuel, is the most difficult of the three to come by. Enough of it has to be applied to the fuel, which is often wet and cold, and maintained long enough to heat the fuel to a temperature at which it will ignite. And then that higher temperature must be maintained long enough for the reaction to sustain itself. In other words, lighting the fire is the most difficult part of the equation—once you get past the point of ignition, it's all downhill. Let's take a look at how to get to that point.

The ability to start a fire, an honored and respected skill for as long as people have lived in or taken to the woods, remains in this day of butane backpacking stoves and electronically lighted camp lanterns as the mark of one who knows his way around the outdoors. It's a badge of competence. Those firmly imbedded in the pour-a-can-of-liquid-firestarter-on-it school of thought can skip this part. As we noted earlier, starting the fire is accomplished by applying enough heat to the fuel to ignite it. Let's take a look at the heat sources.

Matches. Under good conditions, this is probably all you will need. The combination of a kitchen match, plenty of thoroughly dry tinder, and dry sticks on top of the tinder will have you off and running. It almost seems corny, but buy a matchsafe, one of those screwtop metal or plastic tubes, and keep it full and with your gear. You will seldom need it, if ever, but when you do it could be a lifesaver.

An alternative match, impervious to the vagaries of weather, is the *magnesium firestarter*, a pocket-sized block of magnesium with a flint imbedded in one edge. The idea is to shave a small pile of magnesium filings off the block with a knife, then strike the knife against the flint, igniting the magnesium and consequently the tinder which you have carefully and thoughtfully placed over it. Yes, it works. It's a bit hard on the knife, perhaps, and it's an exercise in patience and fortitude. But when matches fail due to the wet, the firestarter comes through.

Many situations, however, call for more than a match. A plain *candle* can often make the difference. It burns for a long time, is lightweight, inexpensive, waterproof, throws enough heat to ignite the most stubborn tinder, is flammable itself, has no moving parts, and is easy to work with. Other additions to the match can include *Sterno* or other brands of canned alcohol pastes which can be scooped out of the can and added to the fire. There's also a similar, and handier, product called *Mautz Fire Ribbon*. It's packaged in a tube and designed for lighting campfires and priming backpacking stoves.

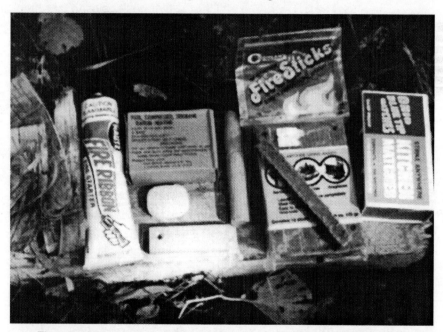

Fire starting aids, left to right: Mautz Fire Ribbon, military surplus trioxane tablets, a magnesium "match," a candle, a commercial compressed wood product starter, and wooden kitchen matches.

An excellent fire-starting material if you come across it is Army surplus *trioxane fuel tabs*. once lighted they burn with an extremely hot, smokeless flame. They perform very well under wet conditions.

One of the best fire-starting aids *is birch bark.* Do not remove this from live trees if you want them to remain alive. In any birch forest there are plenty of down trees from which bark can be peeled.

How to Build a Fire

Though it's already early evening you still have a couple of hours of light left. The day began in brilliant sunshine but a light rain has pursued you on the river all day, with squalls pattering the bow of the canoe and roughening the surface of the water. There is plenty of down wood scattered around your island campsite, though it's damp from the rain of the past week.

You clear an area of pine needles and other debris, and dig a shallow trench wide enough to securely support your metal grill. The trench, along each side, is lined with grapefruit-sized rocks gathered from above the high-water mark of the island. You take your time gathering pencil-sized twigs, being careful to take only those which are off the ground and which are thoroughly dry and grey in color. Accumulating a half-bushel or so of these and storing them under the now beached and overturned canoe, you gather progressively larger sticks, assuring yourself that these are dead branches, and dry-as-possible wood.

Place your candle stub, Sterno, Fire Ribbon, or similar aid in the bottom of the trench. Then lay the smallest of the twigs crosswise across the trench, suspended over the candle or other fire source. Pile more sticks on top of those, but none any larger around than your thumb. With the wet conditions you'll need a hot, strong blaze of tinder before you can commit any larger wood to the fire.

Leaving plenty of open space at each end of the pile of tinder so that oxygen can enter from both ends of the trench, reach in carefully from one end and light the starter. If you have done the rest of the job correctly you will have fire, and you'll be able to feed larger pieces of wood into the fire as it grows.

Wetter conditions than we have illustrated in the above example call for more drastic measures to get that first small batch of tinder started. A gob of canned heat or Fire Ribbon or a trioxane tab would do the trick, if your tinder is of suitable quality. Remember, it can be wet on the surface from rainy conditions, but if it is long-dead, dry wood, it will likely burn. Again, you'll need an adequate initial starter such as the candle, plus dry tinder, and you'll want to have larger pieces of dry wood ready to be added at just the right moment.

The Advantage of Camp Stoves

That works unless the rain has been falling all day. And all last week. Hard. There's about as much chance of finding dry firewood as there is of finding a pair of dry socks. The sleeping bags are dry, snug in their rubberized bags, and there is freeze-dried shrimp creole and other delights packed just for this type of occasion. Time to dig out the camp stove.

When the rain starts the first day into a canoe trip, knowing that you have a backpacker's stove tucked away in your gear will provide considerable peace of mind. It's not going to dry your clothes or provide that cheery warmth and glow that comes with a fire, but at the end of a long, wet day it's a welcome companion. Get a hot meal in you and it will all look better in the morning.

There are as many different stoves on the market as there are tents and hiking boots, and the selection is about as confusing. As we noted earlier, a camp stove certainly won't replace the camp fire but it has its niche, one as important as the open fire. You'll use your stove as a convenience item, getting that quick cup of coffee and hot cereal in the morning, but it will likely also be your backup for times when a fire can't be produced. Your stove may bail out a trip that weather has turned into an exercise in misery, and in an extreme circumstance it could save lives.

The selection of a larger stove, the two- and three-burner models used in established, semi-permanent camps that are reached by vehicle or pack horse, is pretty much nailed down. The only ones I have ever seen are the familiar green Coleman stoves. You'll have to decide exactly how large a model you want, and what type of fuel to burn.

Lighter stoves suitable for the backpacker or canoe camper are another question. The variety of fuels, sizes, types of mechanisms, and rituals practiced to get the things to light requires some consideration in order to match the machine to the situation.

Types of Backpacking Fuels and Stoves

Let's take a look at backpacking stoves first by dividing them by fuel type. A quick count of stoves on the market shows fifteen major models, and I'm certain there will be more next month and next year. Most burn either white gas, kerosene, butane, or alcohol. A couple will burn several of the above fuels in addition to diesel fuel, leaded or unleaded auto gasoline, Stoddard solvent, heating oil, and perhaps whale oil and uranium by now. The list of fuels for the multi-fuel stoves seems to grow yearly. Their weights range from mere ounces to several pounds, and in one configuration or another they're suitable for any type trip imaginable, from Himalayan mountain expeditions to overnighters at the county park. Most of them are terrifically specialized marvels of technology.

The most common stove fuel is white gas, sold as Coleman fuel, Blazo, lantern and stove fuel, and any number of other brand names. Kerosene is used in a few backpacking stoves but hasn't caught on for several reasons that we'll delve into presently. Both white gas and kerosene are purchased in bulk and poured into the stove tank. Cartridge stoves burn either propane or butane from, appropriately, a disposable cartridge that screws onto the burner mechanism of the stove. The few alcohol-burning stoves fill such a specialized and minor niche in the market that we can safely ignore them here.

The pros and cons of the various stove fuels line up like this:

White Gas	Kerosene	Cartridge
Spilled fuel easily evaporates.	Spilled fuel must be wiped up.	Fuel does not spill.
Inexpensive to run.	Inexpensive to run.	Fuel is expensive compared to white gas or kerosene.
Some stoves must be primed to start.	Some stoves must be primed to start.	Instant lighting, no priming.
Will function well in cold weather.	Will function well in cold weather.	Will not function (with few exceptions) under 32° F.

White Gas	Kerosene	Cartridge
Fuel highly flammable—can be a safety concern.	Fuel very safe to use—hard to ignite out of stove.	Caution must be used to avoid leaking cartridges.

There is room for additional comment on the cartridge stoves. On some models the cartridge cannot be removed until empty, requiring the burner-cartridge package to be packed whole, not broken down for easy transport. Others tend to lose pressure, and hence heating efficiency, as the cartridge empties, leaving the camp cook faced with a diminishing burner temperature as the cartridge is used. Finally, some hikers object that the cartridges must be packed out. That's not really a problem, actually, as your fuel bottle for a white gas or kerosene stove must also go home with you.

In defense of the cartridge stove, the convenience cannot be stressed too strongly. Those who use them and restrict that use to short fair-weather trips that require no more than one cartridge will be rewarded with the virtues of instant heat and negligible weight and maintenance problems. Cartridge stoves also have cooked meals and melted snow on top of mountains and under other such adverse circumstances, but such performance seems to be the exception rather than the rule.

How Camp Stoves Work

The majority of stoves you will find in camps are white gas models. While not without drawbacks, as you can see from the preceding chart, they offer advantages unmatched by the cartridge models.

Up to a point, all gasoline and kerosene stoves work the same. Vaporized fuel is fed to the burner under pressure, where this fuel-air mixture burns. The parting of the ways occurs when we look at the manner in which the fuel is pressurized.

Some stoves depend on the fuel tank being warmed, providing pressure from the expanding fuel. The **Svea 123R**, an old and respected stove among backpackers and one of the best-sellers on the market, year in and year out, works on this principle. A small bowl is located just beneath the generator tube on this type of stove.

A small amount of gas is poured into the bowl by the user and ignited, warming the generator and vaporizing enough fuel to start the burner, which then provides the heat to keep the warmed fuel rising to the burner. As you can imagine, the difficulty of the task, negligible in times of pleasant weather, climbs as the temperature falls and the wind howls.

A few popular camp stoves, left to right:
The Svea 123, Coleman Sportster, Coleman Peak 1,
and a Mountain Safety Research fuel bottle.

Stoves such as the **Coleman Peak 1** are equipped with a pump to pressurize the tank, just like the famous green lanterns produced by that outfit, and hence do without the priming bowl and accompanying ritual to provide positive pressure in the fuel tank. Under conditions of extreme cold weather, however, some help is needed in the form of a wad of paper or small amount of fuel which must be ignited under the generator in the same manner as the non-pum-pequipped stoves.

Pump-type stoves are easier to use in the cold. I have left my **Peak 1** in my home freezer for several days at a time and then had it start right up without hesitation.

More time and ink has been expended on what is actually quite a simple task—priming and starting stoves—than the subject probably deserves. While priming gets a little dicey in the cold and rain, some practice at home will provide you with a roaring stove in no time, on command, in the field.

Choosing a stove for your own particular needs is a matter of balancing cost, reliability, availability of parts and service, and the ability of the stove to flawlessly function under inclement weather conditions.

I have used the **Coleman Peak 1** and **Svea 123R** as representative stoves, and I would have to rate the Peak 1 over the lighter Svea if weight were not a factor, or an important factor, and would still opt for the Peak 1 for cold-weather trips as I find it easier to start. other advantages of this stove is that it shares a common fuel with other camp appliances you may use, such as lanterns or catalytic tent heaters. It also functions much like the lantern or larger camp stove and is therefore more familiar and comfortable for the operator to use. It burns very hot when you need the heat and will simmer when you don't (a problem with some stoves is full-blast heat only), and is decidedly windproof due to its four-sided wind guard between the burner and generator.

Caring for Your Stove

Any stove needs some care from time to time. The most common problem with the **Peak 1**, or other pump stoves, is the pump failing to hold pressure. This is easily remedied by squirting a small amount of oil into the hole made for that purpose in the cap over the pump hole in the tank. If this fails, unscrew the pump mechanism after removing the cap and lubricate the leather or rubber washer that is the pump gasket with vegetable oil. Gun oil, saliva, or other field expedients will work when far from home. Eventually the gasket may wear out, at which time the part is easily found at almost any store that carries Coleman stoves or lanterns.

The generators contain a very fine wire that is extended through the fuel orifice when the stove is shut off in order to clean it. This will clog up someday, resulting in generally erratic performance from your stove. This part is also easily found, wherever the stove is sold, and installed with only a wrench.

Filter white gas every time you fill your stove. Use one of the filters with the felt material in the bowl, not just the fine screening, as the felt will deal with the main culprit which is minute amounts of water in the fuel. White gas does not have a long shelf life, so fuel more than a couple of years old should not be used. Likewise, do not leave the tank of the stove full between seasons, as the gas will tend to thicken and gum up orifices and valves.

After purchasing your stove, whatever make and type you decide on, make its maiden voyage in your back yard. Hunkered down behind a canoe in the wind and wet while the stomach shrieks for supper and the soul for a hot drink is not the time to delve into the worldly myster ies of the stove. They each have their idiosyncrasies by type, manufacturer, and individually, and you can come to know these in the wilds of your back yard under much more pleasing circumstances than those described above.

Stove Safety Tips

Stoves are essentially well built, solidly engineered, safe machines, as safe as automobiles, firearms, and electrical appliances. Like these other items, however, backpacking stoves demand respect and caution or they will hurt you. If you will be cooking in your tent, light the stove outside. Fuel spills, overturned stoves, and the occasional and inevitable flare-up that occurs while priming or lighting stoves can turn into a full-scale disaster in the confines of a tent. Keep your face away from—not directly over—the stove when lighting it, for the same reason. Overheating of fuel tanks or cartridges from using oversized cooking pots or too efficient windbreaks can be dangerous. While it is normal for the tank of a gas or kerosene stove to get hot (too hot to touch in some brands), butane or propane cartridges must remain cool to the touch.

Do not use any type of automotive fuel in white gas-only stoves. The additives in the auto fuel will cause you problems down the line, up to and possibly including exploding the stove.

While the fuel tank of your camp stove may allow you to get through a trip without a refill, longer trips call for extra fuel. Cartridge stoves shine here, though remember that the empties must return with you. While camps served by vehicle or pack horse can use gallon cans, the only practical and safe way to carry extra fuel in a pack or canoe is the backpacker's aluminum fuel bottles made by Sigg or Mountain Safety Research. Buy one of the gadgets that fits in the spout and meters the fuel, too. It seems like a small thing, but trying to pour from fuel bottle to stove in the rain without one is an exercise in frustration that ranks right up there with putting on the tent fly after the rain has started.

The Tin Can Hobo Stove

The final stove we'll look at is the original backpacker's home-made stove, known most commonly as the hobo stove. It's been popular among soldiers in every war since the tin can was included in G.I. rations. Like many simple things, it works surprisingly well and has the overwhelming virtue of being cheap, easy to maintain, and disposable.

For those who like to stick to the basics, or for a quick,
overnight trip, the hobo stove is the answer.

After removing both ends from the tin can of your choice, punch a few slots in the bottom with a can opener or knife. Then insert burning matter in the bottom and put dinner on top, and you're in business. Leaving one end partially intact, the end that the cook pan or can will rest on, will provide a more moderate heating surface. This will normally require other than natural materials for fuel due to the small space involved and the need to constantly feed more sticks into the stove if natural fuels are used. Sterno, Fire Ribbon, or a similar substance works great. My favorite is trioxane heat tabs, made for this purpose and available from surplus goods outlets.

We could go on here. We will not. I recommend that the serious, ultra-lightweight backpacker looking for a stove to serve the weight and bulk demands of that calling consult the backpacking literature. Specifically, I highly recommend The Complete Walker III, by Colin Fletcher, for an indepth and amusing look at backpacking stoves and their applications, complete with charts illustrating boiling water times and other esoterica along those lines.

5

Utensils

My first camp cooking utensil was simple and inexpensive. A fifteen-mile Boy Scout hike with a planned meal stop at the mid-point found me broiling chunks of beef on a green stick over a fire. A shaker of salt and pepper and a pocket knife—Boy Scout, of course completed the makings of my "kitchen." I can't say I haven't eaten as well since, but I haven't eaten a whole lot better.

Any method of cooking other than broiling or the traditional heave and scrape method is going to require tools to make it happen. As in any other area of camping or outdoor equipment, the field of writing about camp cooking utensils is pretty crowded. And also as with these other areas, some of the information available is of little practical use to the serious camp cook.

Aluminum—Lightweight but Difficult to Use

Though it's standard procedure to praise aluminum as the saving grace of the backpacker's camp kitchen because of its almost nonexistent weight, the camp cook has to cope with its less-than ideal performance as a cooking utensil. Aluminum is a very efficient conductor of heat—too efficient. For culinary applications this translates into frying pans that develop a "hot spot" in the center of the pan, often burning the portion of the potential meal that is directly in contact with that part of the pan while merely warming through the rest of the contents. It also translates into drinking cups that burn the hand and scorch the lip when hot liquids are imbibed, and into plates that suck the heat from any foods placed on them.

The utensil manufacturers' answer to part of this problem is to coat the insides of frying pans with a non-stick substance like Teflon or Silverstone. Though the main purpose of these coatings is to prevent foods from sticking to the inside of the pan, they also serve to distribute the heat somewhat more evenly across the surface. While this treatment doesn't make the aluminum frying pan the equal of its cousins of iron or steel, the ultra-light backpacker can live with it. Some of these coatings, the early ones in particular, demand special treatment like plastic utensils, while the newer offerings can be abused within reason.

Left to right—a standard camp cook kit coated aluminum pan, a cast-iron pan, and a steel saute pan.

The problems with uncoated aluminum pans have become so familiar that it is difficult to find them for sale these days without the non-stick coating. For many camp cooks, however, a better solution is steel cookware.

A perusal of sporting goods catalogs reveals about as much lightweight steel cookware as aluminum. While it's doubtful that it will ever replace entirely the distinct weight advantage of aluminum, steel is such a step up to quality camp cooking that there are few situations in which I would choose the lighter metal. The finest chefs in the greatest restaurants ply their trade with steel saute pans. The only aluminum cooking utensils you'll find in these kitchens are heavy, up-to-an-inch-thick cast aluminum. When it's this thick, aluminum does an efficient job in some applications as a cooking surface. It also becomes prohibitively heavy, brittle, and expensive.

The Virtues of Stainless Steel Cookware

If you are going shopping for a camp cook kit, be aware that the spread in weight and cost between aluminum and stainless steel is so narrow that I would heartily endorse the steel product. Consulting a camping supply catalog I see a one-person aluminum kit by Mirro and a roughly equivalent kit in stainless steel by Coleman. The price spread between the two is $2.00, and the weight difference is 5 $1/2$ ounces with the advantage going to the steel. This is due in this case to the slightly smaller capacities of the Coleman product and its lack of a carrying case. Another comparison, between compatible twoperson stainless steel and aluminum sets both manufactured by Mirro, has a $1.00 spread in price and almost identical weights.

Stainless steel frying pans don't normally carry a non-stick inner surface as do their aluminum counterparts, but neither is the need as great. The almost-universal application of Teflon or its brothers on the aluminum pans is because no matter how careful you are, you will likely burn anything thicker than water to the bottom of the pan. Thin steel is almost as bad in this department, so the stainless steel pans usually have a copper coating applied to the outside surface. This is the treatment applied to premium-quality "gourmet" cookware, and it works. The copper spreads the heat evenly enough that the thickness of the steel can be kept to backpacking-weight levels.

The Cast-Iron Frying Pan

The quality of camp cookware generally improves as it gains weight. The classic camp cooking utensil of the "old days," the beans, bacon, and bannock days, was the cast-iron frying pan, or "spider." With this versatile tool one can do an unexcelled job on anything from baking bread to frying eggs over-easy to deep-fried fish fillets due to cast iron's superior heat-retaining ability. Many cooks, both indoor and out, have gone full circle. They started with the old black pans, then they flirted with aluminum, steel, and the coated steel products, only to find that none of them, even with their hightech glitter, produce as consistently fine results as cast iron.

The tradeoff, of course, is the weight. Cast iron is a brittle, fragile metal, and to make it sturdy enough for even casual use the metal must be thick enough to make up for this weakness. Unless you're on a canoe trip with few portages or camping out of a vehicle, the "Spider" will have to stay home.

The Steel Restaurant Saute Pan

Another item which definitely has an application in the kitchen of camp cooks is the steel (not stainless) restaurant saute pan. This is professional restaurant equipment and will have to be purchased in a restaurant supply store, easily found in any fair-sized city. The saute pan is a compromise, falling into a niche between the cast iron frying pan and the lightweight camp cookware-set pans. It is made of thick enough steel to provide even heat when frying over a fire without the excess weight of the cast iron pan. The cost is not excessive, and these work out so well in camp, particularly over a gasoline stove, that the effort of finding them is well worth it.

Plastic Utensils

Plastic has probably made a greater contribution to camp eating utensils than has aluminum. Plastic cups, plates, and bowls weigh no more than aluminum, they don't dent when dropped (resulting in repairs having to be made with a rock or hammer to get them to nest), don't conduct scorching heat to your lips in the wee, dark hours from your morning cup of hot chocolate or coffee, and they cost less. Every camp cook kit that I have seen presently on the market now sports plastic cups, bowls, and plates exclusively.

With the exception of the materials from which cooking and eating utensils are manufactured, little has changed from the last century.

The naturalist Nessmuk, speaking in the classic *Woodcraft*, lists his camp kit as a set of "tinware," or light steel, dishes, five in number, which nest together with the smaller serving as lids for the larger. He only took this amount of cookware along to more permanent camps, however. His solitary, Spartan treks through the wilderness often required only a single steel bowl.

Another classic American outdoor camp chef, Horace Kephart, reported in *Camp Cookery* in 1959 that he used about the same amount of dishes as Nessmuk, which pretty much resembled a modern-day cook kit with the exception of the materials of which it was manufactured. Even at this early date Kephart had little good to say about aluminum. He recommended "enamelware," a coated steel seldom seen these days, having been largely replaced with plastic.

Furnishing Your Camp Kitchen

Considering the variety of types of utensils available to the camp cook—from plastic or coated aluminum and copper-clad stainless steel to the cast iron frying pan—where do you start furnishing your camp kitchen?

The answer depends, of course, on your type of camp and how you are carrying your utensils. The ultralight backpacker, subsisting on freeze-dried and dehydrated foods, will do quite well with one of the aluminum or stainless steel kits designed for this type of activity. Two pots for boiling water and a plastic bowl, spoon, and cup will do an adequate job while adding minimal weight to the load carried on the back for those eating out of plastic pouches.

Canoe trip and permanent camp cooks can pay less attention to weight and more accumulating a set of cooking utensils that will allow one to pursue some of the diverse avenues of eating that we are exploring in this book. This doesn't mean that the entire contents of your kitchen, perhaps with the exception of the sink, need to be trundled off to the bush every weekend. The idea is to have a minimal amount of carefully selected tools to work with—tools that will seve you in preparing meals rather than you serving them by spending an inordinate amount of effort hauling them all around. Kephart sums this up in *Camp Cookery*, saving that "Ideal outfitting

Aluminum utensils still form the bulk of many camp cook kits.

is to have what we want, when we want it, and never to be bothered with anything else."

One problem with buying one of the standard camp cook kits on the market is that parts of it won't fit your needs. The kettles are too small or too large. The coffee pot is too small. Or to get the sizes you need you have to buy a kit for six, and there are only four of you in camp. You may find yourself buying two or more kits, or better yet, picking up what you need at flea markets, rummage sales, and second-hand shops.

Sometimes even this tactic backfires. Mike, one of the deer camp regulars, had his wife constantly scouting rummage sales for sporting goods, including camp cooking utensils. As anything she found used kept him out of the sporting goods stores and catalogs where things begin to cost real money, her heart was in the job. I was visiting the day she presented him with a like-new coffee percolator, purchased at a rummage sale for next to nothing. After thanking her Mike casually, without a second thought, removed the inner basket and stem and flipped them into the trash can. We boil our coffee the old way in camp. Mike couldn't understand the horrified look on her face until she explained that she had searched for weeks for a complete pot because all of the numerous others she had seen were missing the insides. Of such things are happy marriages made.

Putting together a set of camp cooking tools is one of those definitive expressions of personal taste. But for an example, here is what I usually have in one of mine.

> 1 large, restaurant-type meat fork
> 1 metal spatula
> 1 slotted spoon
> 3 aluminum pots with lids—4 quart, 3 quart,
>   1 cast-iron skillet
> 1 Dutch oven
> 1 set of plates, bowls, and cups for 4
> 1 set of plastic forks and spoons for 4
> 1 heavy metal grate for the fire

A camp cook kit such as this one will provide for several people, but you may want to add to it in the form of cast iron frying pans or perhaps plastic plates to replace the aluminum.

That is a heavy outfit and is carried by pickup truck, not back or canoe. For canoe trips I pack the following.

    1 large spoon
    1 heavy steel saute pan (frying pan) instead of the
       cast iron pan
    2 aluminum pots with lids—2 quart and 1 quart
       1 plastic bowl for mixing and marinating
    1 plastic bowl and spoon for each person
    1 reflector oven
    1 backpacker's lightweight fire grate

This outfit is versatile enough to produce near anything we will deal with in this book, and light enough to hump across the sweatiest, most mosquito-bitten portages you are likely to encounter.

In both cases knives are not included as there are always enough personal knives in camp. The use of plates when you are trying to watch the weight of your outfit, as in the canoe tripper's kitchen above, is superfluous when a bowl will serve the same function.

At least one of the cups in each kit serves as a measuring cup. If it isn't marked when purchased, measure a half cup of water into it and mark both that point and the full cup point with the tip of a knife blade. Similarly, the spoons are either about tablespoon size or teaspoon sized, checked at home against a measuring spoon set, saving the weight and space of carrying additional measuring cups and spoons.

Mess Kits

G.I. surplus cooking utensils are advertised here and there for camping purposes. I have had less than good luck with these. The U.S. mess kit, though it appears to be a plate-frying pan combination, is actually two steel plates, one with a divider, designed for carrying through chow lines. They are not carried in the field or cooked with. Attempts to cook with the "frying pan" deliver the same results as with any other uncoated or unplated thin steel or aluminum pan: burnt food at the point where the heat touches the metal. Actually, I can't imagine anyone wanting to use a utensil that is produced by an organization (the U.S. Army) that has earned a solid reputation for over two hundred years for its terrible food. Think about it.

The German Army mess kit, found on the surplus market from time to time at a very attractive price, is of an entirely different philosophy. Designed not only for walking through the mess lines, the lower portion of the kit is a deep kidney-shaped pail for heating ration cans in boiling water. For overnight trips when I don't want to get too fancy with meal preparation I have used mine both with

The West German Army mess kit, shown on the left,
is more useful in camp than the U.S. model.

regular canned items and with the retort pouch "canned" foods that we will discuss later in this book. Your supper or lunch packs right in the mess kit and the empties can be packed out inside it. Remember that if you heat canned foods, you must punch a hole in the can to release the expanding steam. This is critical when heating directly over flames, but even double-boiled cans can yield a painful surprise if this precaution is ignored.

Camp Dishwashing

Dishwashing in camp can be as easy or complicated as you make it. First off, accept the fact (and enjoy it as an indication of your growing outdoor veteran status) that your brand-new shiny pot and pan set is going to slowly turn black from soot whether you cook over a fire or a stove. Those who are compulsively neat can resort to soaping the bottoms of cooking pots before consigning them to the flames. This prevents the buildup of soot and ash by creating a unique new mess of burnt up soap, soot, and ash mixed together.

Give a perfunctory wipe to nesting pots and stuff the blackened utensils in a stuff sack and forget them. Allow yourself the smug satisfaction of knowing that by leaving the outside of the pots black they are now more efficient over the flames, not having that intense reflective surface.

The logical item that comes to mind for camp dish cleanup is the soap-impregnated steel wool pad—until you use one. The massive quantities of soap suds that ooze out of these things is as much of a chore to clean up afterwards as whatever it was you burnt onto the pan in the first place, and they tend to shed fine steel shavings throughout everything they come in contact with.

In every restaurant I was employed by during my career as a chef, the bottom rung of the social ladder was always occupied by the dishwashers. That is why the most devastating insult a cook could receive was for one of these generally overworked and underpaid gentlemen to walk up to the cooking line, hands grasping a stock pot or saute pan with a charred, blackened mess burnt to the bottom, and ask him if he knows how to cook. Take care to watch your heat during the cooking process and you'll not only enjoy a better tasting meal, but you'll also save yourself a lot of work at the end. The dishwasher, in camp, is you.

If you pack a plastic or coarse steel wool scrub pad and a small plastic bottle of dishwashing soap you'll have the necessary tools to take care of all your dishwashing chores. To speed things along, at the close of each meal toss the dirty dishes into the largest pot you have and boil. This treatment will do most of the work for

*This is the dishwashing gear provided with one of the aluminum field kitchens from **Camper's Kitchen**.*
It's a little fancy for my taste, but some will appreciate it.

you,and a second pot of boiling water will do the job of rinsing off the soap and sanitizing your utensils of bacteria. Bar soap also works just fine for dishwashing if you carry it for yourself anyway.

Sand is the traditional dishwashing medium and it is far from obsolete. This won't do for non-stick coatings on frying pans, but does just as good a job on everything else as it has been doing since the invention of plates.

A safe, environmentally sound manner of disposing of dishwashing water is to pour it into a hole which is covered with a layer of dirt each time it is used and filled when camp is vacated. Grease from cooking can go in this same hole, as well as any organic garbage that has first been burned, such as bones.

Grates

All of these cooking utensils are of no use over an open fire unless you have a suitable grate to rest them on. Once again the permanent camp, with little in the way of weight restrictions, can be equipped with ease-of-use and convenience as first priority and weight and bulk second. Don't pay money for a heavy grate. The shelves from old ovens, those from commercial models being the best as they are heavier and larger, can be acquired without too much trouble if you keep your eyes open, and grates from rusted-out charcoal grills will work equally well. Avoid most refrigerator shelving as the metal coating found on some of them can be toxic.

A metal grate is superior to most of the contraptions illustrated in outdoor cooking books such as the dingle stick, with which a pot is supported by a stick rammed into the ground and supported by a rock, the whole business dependent on the placid nature of the cook fire and the cook's good judgment as to the strength of the stick. Or the wooden pot-hanger constructions which support pots over the fire, the height adjusted by moving the pots up and down on wooden "S" hooks whittled from trees. The grate offers the camp cook a firm, flat, solid surface to work on. By regulating the fire with a hot side and cold side, you can broil on one end of the grate while the coffee cooks in the middle and your pot of gravy simmers at the other end.

Take pains to build your fire with your grate in mind. The primary purpose of lighting the fire in the first place is to cook on. If it is too wide for the grate, or otherwise shaped wrong to support it, you'll either have to start over and rebuild the fire lay or change it while the fire is burning. Or you can just lay the grate across the fire, supported in a half-hearted manner by a log here and a rock there, and hope that it can ignore the laws of gravity until at least after dinner. Just hope.

The canoe camper or backpacker who wishes to cook over a wood fire can either adopt grates from the smaller models of charcoal grills or, better yet, purchase a folding or collapsible grate. These either have legs which fold underneath the grate or are in the form of hollow, telescoping, stainless steel tubing that extends to form a grate large enough for a cook pot or two and collapses to fit in a backpack or canoe grub box.

A backpacker's folding grate fits easily in pack or canoe camper's gear.

Your choice of utensils can make or break your camp cooking experience. A co-worker related to me how he and a few friends had switched from tents and an outdoor kitchen on their annual fishing trip to Ontario to a rented motor home, complete with microwave oven and air conditioning. He agreed that they had lost a part of the trip, every year since, by being cooped up in their metal box instead of outdoors with the owls hooting at night and the loons laughing in the morning.

When pressed for an explanation, he stressed that they had become fed up with trying to cook on "one of those gasoline stoves that gave them nothing but burnt food." I wonder how much of that problem had to do with some discount store aluminum cook kit and the lack of a little knowledge of practical camp cooking.

6

Carrying It

Everything tastes better cooked in camp, whether it's prepared over flickering flames and popping coals or the tiny, urgent roar of a backpacking stove. I'm not sure if this is because of the atmosphere of the outdoor "dining room" or due to the seasoning of wood smoke and ashes, a little sand or dirt, and any members of the insect community that fly too low over the pot.

But to cook in camp you need a kitchen. The farther you travel from your home kitchen, the more difficult it becomes to prepare anything more ambitious than the creeping tedium of countless cans of pork and beans or an eternity of burgers on the grill.

Pre-packed Camp Kitchen

Your camp kitchen can vary in form from a stuff sack or two riding in a backpack to a massive wooden or metal chest of drawers and shelves. But the basic idea is the same—to have a container in which your camp cooking gear, a few herbs and spices, and some staple foods can be stored ready for use. To pack all the needed items for a trip from memory or a list every time you leave is only to guarantee that something will be left behind. In particular, you will jeopardize your ability to take advantage of foods offered by nature, as you'll have forgotten the cornmeal for fried bluegills or the spices for a crayfish boil.

If you are both a lightweight-backpacking or canoe camper and also a visitor to campgrounds accessible by vehicle, your best bet is to make up two kitchens and leave them packed and ready to go. You can do more with your larger outfit, of course, though much of the space is taken up by the two-burner gasoline stove, eating utensils for five, a Dutch oven, several cast iron frying pans, and other permanent camp kitchen equipment. The small, backpack-sized kitchen actually takes more work in the planning stage as its size precludes tossing in whatever meets your fancy at the time, a luxury you can get away with in the larger model.

Suggested Light-weight Kitchen

The ultra-lightweight backpacker willing to restrict his diet to freeze dried or dehydrated foods can trim his load back to almost nothing. In fact, a knife, spoon, plastic bowl or large cup, and pot to cook in will do it. Serious eating, however, and being able to take advantage of a larger variety of plant and animal food that you may encounter on your trip requires a little more. The goal in putting together the lightweight kitchen is to balance weight and bulk with utility—the kitchen should have sufficient utensils, spices and staples. But it shouldn't be such a burden to carry that you find yourself trimming it before each trip or leaving entire parts of it home.

Your kitchen, of whatever size, will change with the number of trips you take, and it will reflect the type of cooking you do. Starting out with a basic kit for backpacking or canoeing demands that you begin small. While you can begin with everything up to and including (almost) the kitchen sink when your trips involve transportation by vehicle, the foot trail or portage is not the place to test your ability as a pack animal. Start out with a very basic outfit like the one below or the simple kit in the previous chapter. The two emergency meals mentioned stay in my kit at all times. Freeze-dried foods are ideal for this duty, supplying a hedge against either inclement weather that keeps you afield for a day longer than planned, or just the freedom to stay another night if the trip is a particular treasure.

Basic Backpacking Kitchen

1 plastic drinking cup
1 plastic high-sided bowl
1 one quart cook pot with lid

1 frying pan
1 spoon
1 garbage bag
Matches
A pot scrubber and soap (or use hand soap)
Margarine in squeeze tube or other suitable container
2 emergency meals

You can eat with this kit. Not particularly well, as this outfit depends on a good quantity of freeze-dried or canned foods; it is basically set up for boiling water and heating pre-cooked meals. A more versatile outfit that will allow you some latitude in your camp dining and free you from total dependence on the foil pouch follows:

Canoe Trip or Backpacking Kitchen

1 plastic bowl
1 plastic cup
1 spoon
1 one-quart pot with lid
1 two-quart pot with lid
1 frying pan
1 can opener
Matches
Pot scrubber and soap
1 garbage bag
A selection of spices in 35 mm film containers
Cooking oil
Cornmeal
Chicken and beef bouillon cubes or base
2 emergency meals

The following items are in my lightweight kitchen. I backpack little, most of my non-permanent camp trips being by canoe, and this may be a bit heavy for the serious packer. In addition to the items listed above, I take these supply items along:

Canoe Kitchen

Lemon juice
Instant oatmeal
Brown sugar
Bannock mix
Rice
Dry egg noodles or macaroni
Shortening

The instant oatmeal and brown sugar are my standard fishing trip and deer-camp breakfast. It's fast, no hassle, reasonably nutritious, and inexpensive. Another trip standard mentioned in the above list is bannock, which we examine in detail in the chapter on baking. I keep several plastic bags of the premixed, dry bannock mix in the canoe kitchen. With the addition of shortening, which doubles as frying oil on these trips, and water, I have fresh baked bread in camp, and the dry mix is an ingredient for a fried fish batter.

Special Containers

Zip-lock plastic bags are a major tool of the backpacker and canoe camper. The sandwich sizes may need some tape to reinforce the seal while being bounced around in a pack. The muscular quart and gallon sizes can transport a substantial load, such as your fireblackened cooking pots. These bags will fulfill a large portion of your food-packing requirements.

Peruse the Tupperware or similar plastic food storage container possibilities. Many of these are admirably suited to the camp kitchen, and the price is right. other possibilities are the food containers designed for the backpacker and sold in backpacking, sporting goods, and some department stores, or through the mail from any camping supply distributor. These include wide- and narrow-mouth plastic jars of various capacities with screw tops, reusable plastic toothpaste-type tubes for margarine, jelly, or whatever else of a similar consistency strikes your fancy, flasks for liquid foodstuffs or libations, and a multitude of more specialized containers such as the egg holder that cradles each egg in its own cozy compartment, all made of reasonably indestructible plastic.

35 mm film containers perform well for storing spices and small amounts of items like soup bases, flour, or oil for frying. Label them with masking tape and procure some type of container to prevent them from surprise openings. I use a pouch manufactured by Safariland designed to carry 35 mm film containers of deer urinesoaked cotton to mask a hunter's scent. The pouch holds each container in an elastic band with larger bands for other items. These pouches are much easier to find than the backpacker's nylon kitchen pouches, and are usually drastically more reasonable in price.

Chest-type Kitchens

Going from a soft, backpack-type kitchen to a hard-sided footlocker or chest-type outfit means that you can get serious about cooking in camp. Though the present-day outfitted canoe trips in the north-woods provide the camper with a food pack containing a supply of freeze-dried food and a utensil set, the traditional kitchen is the wanigan. The wanigan is a wooden (or in my updated case, aluminum), box hinged at the top containing food, cooking utensils, and perhaps a small stove. Most have backpack straps attached to one side for carrying over portages. While the Dutch oven is still too heavy for most canoe trips, the wanigan will digest with ease a reflector oven, a cast-iron frying pan, and other tools of quality outdoor cooking.

The traditional wooden wanigan isn't offered for sale anywhere I have looked, but an aluminum equivalent, manufactured by Camper's Kitchen of San Antonio, Texas, does a great job. It has the advantage of lighter weight and a reflective surface to keep the contents a bit cooler in the heat of the summer. The Camper's Cupboard, as this model is called, lacks the pack straps of the wooden wanigan and some of its sturdiness. I have used a tumpline or a clip-on shoulder strap to carry mine. That's helped me avoid dropping it on rocks, ramming it into trees, and similar canoe portage abuse.

The contents of the wanigan are the same as those mentioned earlier in the canoe- and backpacking-kitchen lists, with the addition of my reflector oven, a cast iron frying pan, and such luxuries as forks and a spatula. Spices and other non-perishable foods can be packed in somewhat larger quantities, sparing you the job of completely restocking your inventory after each trip. I keep a running list on a scrap of paper right in the wanigan of those items that will need refilling upon my return home. Repacking the kitchen immediately will have it ready for the next opportunity, however fleeting, to get out of town.

There are other avenues available to the canoe camper who can't or would rather not construct a canoe camp kitchen. There are

Make your kitchen large enough to hold a selection of spices and staple items. This way, only perishables need to be packed for a camping trip.

*This aluminum camp kitchen carries a complete
selection of utensils, stove, and foods.*

*The aluminum wanigan will hold all the gear
needed for cooking, plus some food items.*

footlockers and such on the market, as well as some large tool boxes, that will do the job. Take along a set of measurements of the inside width of your canoe when you go shopping.

Kitchens for permanent or vehicle-served camps can pretty much forget about being concerned with weight and size and concentrate on including all the utensils and staple foods for some real gourmet camp cooking. If you are handy with tools (or have a brother-in-law who is), make a list of the items you will want to keep in the kitchen, pile them up in the garage to see how large a structure you will need, and design your kitchen using the photographs in this chapter as a source of ideas. Allowing room to store and use a camp stove right in the kitchen is a nice touch, and provides a surface to work on.

Keep in mind the vehicle your kitchen will be transported in. I neglected to measure the height of my pickup truck when I built my first one, it was only luck that it cleared the roof of the cab by an inch.

I recommend heavy lumber—one by ones for the framing and half-inch plywood for the sides and bottom. You will have a lot of weight in the box and it's going to bounce around in the back of a pickup truck, get rained on, sit in a damp corner of the garage when not in use, and be subject to other maltreatment that will be the early death of any flimsy construction.

Sturdy construction is recommended if you build your own kitchen.

The do-it-yourselfer who likes to work from a more formal plan can get full-scale plans for camp kitchens ranging from a simple box with a fold-down front and some shelves to an ornate, complete "outdoor

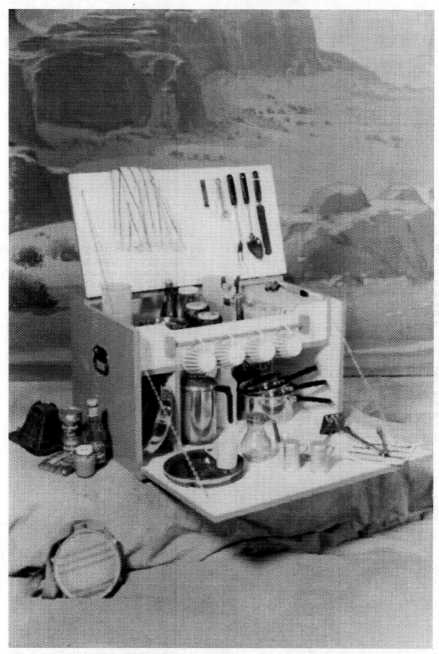

This canoe-sized camp kitchen can be built using your materials and plans from U-Bild. (Photo courtesy of U-Bild.)

Another camp kitchen, this one designed for the permanent camp, from plans supplied by U-Bild. (Photo courtesy of U-Bild.)

One of the camp kitchens that can be built from plans
purchased from U-Bild (Photo courtesy U-Bild.)

kitchen" featuring storage compartments for foodstuffs and a stove, fold-out surfaces for cooking and eating, and removable legs. The whole business folds up to fit into the trunk of a large car. Plans are available from U-Bild Enterprises, Box 2383, Van Nuys, California 91409.

Camper's Kitchen also makes a larger model, the Camper's Kitchen Deluxe. Equipped with a complete set of cooking, eating, and cleaning up utensils, the deluxe model will set you back a few dollars but in one purchase you are ready, with the addition of your herb and spice rack, a few staples, and a cast iron or steel frying pan, for camp. The Deluxe will provide you with such non-essentials as two dish pans, a drying rack, and a set of measuring spoons, among others. You will want to go through it and pare some of the "deadwood" to make room for your Dutch oven and some of the other items we have covered.

Caring for Perishable Foods

Carrying perishable foods is a whole different set of problems. The cooking oil and rice in your kitchen can be packed and forgotten until needed in camp, but most meats, eggs, fresh vegetables, and other perishables need special handling, and not just in the heat of the summer months. Campers enjoying the winter have the same problem in reverse—that of protecting foods from freezing.

Let's look at refrigeration first. The obvious answer is to pack one of the various types of insulated coolers with ice. For permanent camps, no problem. As we travel lighter, however, the weight and bulk of the cooler become unacceptable. Though I have seen coolers carried in canoes, the occupants have either been novices or were not traveling much farther than an overnight stay. The usual routine is to freeze fresh meats, wrap them in heavy foil, and to use these items first, finishing up the trip with dehydrated, canned, or other weather-proof foods. Even ground beef can be carried in the summer months without the benefit of a cooler if you are careful to use it before it reaches 40° F. or above.

The life of perishable foods can be stretched further during periods of warm weather by using a canvas or burlap bag soaked in water. Place the foods you wish to keep cold, still in their containers, in a canvas or burlap bag. Then either dip the bag in a stream or lake or douse it with water from a canteen and hang the bag in the shade. The evaporation produces a refrigeration effect that will cool the contents, not to the degree that they will at home in a refrigerator, but enough to do the job in camp. This method works—don't take my word for it, ask any old midwestern farmer who used to keep a canvas water bag spiked with a few drops of lemon juice hanging in a shade tree while he did the plowing.

A nearby stream, if the water flowing in it is cooler than the air temperature, can also be used for camp refrigeration. Place foods in their containers in a burlap sack, a mesh onion sack, or other similar container, fastening the bag to a tree branch or rock. Be aware that raccoons and other night stalkers like to prowl stream and river banks. Take precautions by using sturdy, well-sealed bags.

If you do use a cooler, it will serve you as well in November when the mercury dips below the freezing mark as it did on that sweaty bass fishing excursion in mid-July. People forget that insulation works in both directions. Not only will it keep the heat out of the cooler in the warmer months, it will keep it inside when you need it during the winter months as well.

Though it is common knowledge that certain foods (fresh vegetables and fresh eggs, for instance) should not be allowed to freeze, most camp cooks don't know that you can get away with freezing them once. Anything from stalks of celery to onions to the dozen eggs that you packed can be allowed to freeze if you cook them directly from the frozen state. Thawing vegetables will leave you with a mushy, unpalatable mess, but cooking them directly from frozen is similar to working with canned products. Likewise eggs can be cracked and cooked from frozen (scrambled only, of course) with no ill effects other than the slight inconvenience.

Canned foods won't freeze at the same temperature as water due to their high salt content, but if they do freeze use them in that state. Frozen and subsequently thawed canned goods should be discarded.

The original camp cooler is simply a hole in the ground. This will prevent water supplies from freezing on the coldest winter day, providing the hole is deep enough, and will provide a modicum of refrigeration in the summer months. Manage your hole-in-the-ground coolers depending on conditions. You may want to leave a water jug storage hole uncovered during a sunny winter day, for instance, as the sun will heat the water and retain that heat after you cover the hole to hold it in through the night. Likewise, keep your subterranean cooler covered during the daylight hours on a hot summer's day, opening it only when necessary during the cooler hours of the day.

Precautions Against Animal Intruders

The local wildlife may dictate the method of natural refrigeration that you adopt in your camp. In bear country, food is kept out of tents used for sleeping and is hoisted out of reach at times when camp is empty. The hole-in-the-ground system is clearly not the answer under these conditions, but the wet bag cooler will work if you are careful to locate it where it can remain in the shade throughout the day. The bag needs to be wet down more than once in the morning as the evaporation that creates the cooling effect also dries the bag, so noon lunches back in camp are in order.

Skunks, porcupines, various ground and tree squirrels, raccoons, black bears, and opossums invite themselves to dinner in your camp at the first opportunity you provide. There are various health threats from animals of which you should be aware. The rabies threat from skunk populations is so great in some areas that health departments consider all skunks to be rabid and urge people to avoid them more for that reason than the obvious. A parasite that attacks the brain and optic nerve cells of humans is found in raccoon feces. I would be the last person to try and separate the camper from the wild world—that is why we are out there in the first place. But humans and these other species are just not made to live together in the same camp. Keeping them out of the camp by using proper food storage methods will be doing both yourself and them a service.

The very best reason for putting together a kitchen or two for your camping trips is that you will find those trips becoming more frequent. The less work it takes to get you out of the house and into the woods for a weekend, the more likely you will go. The camp kitchen makes this a matter of throwing it, the tent and sleeping bags, and some personal gear in the car or truck, stopping at the store for a few things on the way out, and you're gone. No more tearing through the garage and shed looking for this pan or the stove—just the thought of one of those routines on a Friday afternoon is enough to make anyone give up and warm up the VCR. Don't forget to go back to work on Monday.

7

The Fireside Bakery

Some major differences come to light when we compare the great outdoor cookbooks of yesteryear with many of the books written today. One is that the modern books don't assume that there will be a constant supply of freshly obtained fish and game, which is understandable in these urban times. A continuing succession of camp deer or a steady supply of trout to feed the camp would be irresponsible, if not illegal, today. The other difference is the lack of discussion of camp baking. There's little instruction in the preparation of breads, biscuits, and so forth over the fire, though this is the second-oldest cooking skill of mankind after broiled meat.

Perhaps part of the reason that camp baking has become somewhat of a lost art is the way in which some writers handled the subject in the past. One of my favorite references for doing just about anything in camp (except baking, as we will see) is *Woodcraft*, by Nessmuk. Sandwiched between tales of being surrounded by great flocks of wild turkeys and of tramping through the wilderness of southern Michigan for ten days without seeing another human (hard to do for ten minutes in that area today), he talks about food and cooking quite a bit.

Nessmuk's tastes in camp baking run to the far end of simple, a mere step away from gnawing the raw grain off the stalk. The flapjack, or pancake, is too complicated and civilized for Nessmuk, "I do not like it; I seldom make it; it is not good," who prefers the dish that is perhaps responsible for the demise of campfire baking in this country: Johnnycake.

Johnnycake, according to Nessmuk, is a mixture of cornmeal and water, considered a good carp bait in some parts of the country, with a touch of salt or sugar. You can boil the mixture first before baking, or just mix and put it in the pan. At any rate, it doesn't rate. It's not cornbread, and it just isn't very good. Nessmuk himself didn't exactly praise his bakery as the last word in camp food, saying only, "It makes wholesome, palatable bread, which gains on the taste with use." We can do better.

Once past the Johnnycake we can take a balanced look at camp baking. The only thing on Earth more desirable than fresh baked goods coming out of the oven at home is the same thing in camp.

The basic tools of the fireside baker—reflector oven,
dutch oven, and cast iron frying pan.

As cooking with real fire and being in camp makes everything else you eat taste better, a frying pan bread or simple biscuit takes on legendary status.

The first simple bannock I turned out of a frying pan in deer camp drew a response from the rest of the group far out of proportion to the difficulty of producing it. Since that snowy evening meal many seasons ago we have graduated to biscuits, dumplings, fruit tarts, cornbread, and an occasional baked treat at breakfast.

Camp Baking Techniques

Before we look at recipes, let's look at technique. As in any other branch of outdoor cooking, once you get a few ways and means of baking under your belt, starting with the simpler baking powder and corn breads, the rest will come easily. Though literally anything that can be baked can be done in camp over or in your fire, we aren't living under canvas for the purpose of opening a bakery. We'll stick to those baked goods that will add a new dimension to the outing rather than take away from it by harnessing you to the fireside and recipe book.

For the same reason that the very first food you probably cooked at home was a boiled hot dog, we will start with a Johnnycake, baked in a frying pan. It's so simple that with little effort you will have a finished bread which will taste good because you made it, though it won't place in the Betty Crocker Bakeoff. I make no promises for subsequent use of that recipe, but who knows? Perhaps it will "gain on the taste with use," as it did with George.

Breads for camp can be divided into those raised with baking powder and those prepared with yeast. Yeast-risen breads in camp are normally sourdough, which is some of the most wonderful tasting stuff you will ever come across but is somewhat of a bother in camp. Either the weather has to be quite warm or you need a heated tent or cabin with a constant temperature for the yeast to work overnight. Waking up expecting a risen sourdough "sponge" and finding instead a funny looking flour soup is not my idea of starting the day out on the right side of the sleeping bag. I make sourdough at home or in places that include permanent shelters, or during summer fishing trips when I'm not catching much and I need something to boost a flagging ego. There's nothing like turning out a stack of sourdough flapjacks onto another fisherman's plate to brand yourself "woodsman."

Learning to Judge Heat Levels

Once ingredients have been put together to form a batter, loaf, or whatever, it has to have heat applied to it in just the right way to make it raise without becoming a scale model of a charcoal briquette. Baking requires the application of rather intense heat in such a manner that it is evenly distributed. You're not going to have any thermometers or thermostats plugged into the side of your Dutch oven or frying pan, so starting with your first Johnnycake you will begin to develop a "feel" for the amount of heat being transferred from fire to food.

There are various formulas for measuring this, from counting the number of coals or charcoal briquettes placed on a Dutch oven lid to holding your hand in front of the fire and counting the seconds required for it to become uncomfortable, none of which work well unless used under the same conditions each time. The formulas are okay as a guide, but as you learn that the wind velocity and temperature, type of wood used on your fire, presence or absence of reflective material and many other factors influence the amount of heat absorbed by your cooking utensil, you will depend more on experience gained and become a better camp chef because of it. It's not as difficult as it may sound. Your great-grandmother, or perhaps grandmother, depending on your particular family history, baked this way every day.

Cooking Bread in a Frying Pan

The basic utensil of the camp baker is the frying pan. Cast iron is best for baking but the steel frying pan served generations of out-doorsmen and is the utensil of choice for the weight conscious camper. There is a world of difference between the two so if possible choose one and stick with it. About all you will bake in the frying pan is a ban-nock, the most simple of baking-powder breads and a staple in the diet of trappers, lumberjacks, and other outdoorsmen of the last century.

The cast iron pan will heat up slowly, gently, and evenly over the fire and will retain that heat. The steel pan will get hot at the point where the most heat is applied and remain comparatively cool in other spots. Try for even heat, rotating the pan periodically while baking. The expert campfire baker will only have to move the pan once, but don't be afraid to turn it more often in the beginning. Here the heavy-steel restaurant saute pan really shines.

The cast iron frying pan is the traditional camp baking utensil.

When using the frying pan for a simple bannock or cornbread you can cover it with a lid or metal plate and heap coals on top to make a miniature oven, though the traditional method is to bake the bottom side over the coals and then lean the pan against a rock or stump by the fire to allow the top to cook by direct radiant heat. Either way works. Or just turn it over in the pan like a big pancake. But do it gently—

an airborne flip will knock the wind out of your bread and make it heavy and pasty.

Cooking Breads in a Dutch oven

While the Dutch oven is best known for the great way it treats beans, it really comes into its own in the bakery department. Anything you can do in a frying pan, and even in your oven at home, will be better in the Dutch oven due to its small size and thick, heatsaving cast-iron construction. The overturned Dutch oven lid is like a super cast-iron frying pan with its massive weight and bulk.

If possible, dig a hole to one side of your fire pit for the dutch oven.

The main stumbling block experienced in using the Dutch oven for baking is not getting it hot enough. Remember that you are dealing with one heck of a good sized chunk of cast iron which must absorb enough heat to get it hot before passing any of that heat along to your potential bread. I like to pile on the coals when I start assembling ingredients for whatever baked goods I'm planning for dinner. By the time I have them sorted out, the oven is hot. I find that if you concentrate on getting heat to the top of the oven by piling extra coals on the lid that the bottom usually takes care of itself.

The length of time to wait before peeking into the oven is determined in the same manner as the correct heat: by experience. Removing the lid too often will cool your bread or biscuits too much for them to bake, and waiting too long will cause a problem in the opposite direction. other than the temperature of the fire and type of coals (hardwood coals burn considerably hotter), other factors that will affect your cooking time are the temperature of the batter or dough when it's placed in the oven, the air temperature, and the degree of accuracy you applied in adding the liquid part of the recipe. Drier batters and doughs cook faster.

When baking in the Dutch oven, concentrate on heating the top.

Cooking Breads in a Reflector oven

The reflector is probably the easiest baking tool for the newcomer to learn as you can watch your bread baking without worrying about losing heat by removing the lid. They do require quite a healthy fire, however, and for this reason are left at home on trips where large fires are impractical.

Use the reflector oven in the mornings, when the press of getting ready for the day's activities makes food that can be watched from across the campsite a necessity and the liberal blaze used to shake off that morning chill can be put to good use. A bannock with some chocolate beverage powder mixed into it and topped with some canned or

Baking in the reflector oven requires a hot, open fire.

reconstituted dry fruits is about the best way there is to begin a day in the woods or on the water.

Keep the inside of your reflector oven shiny, as even a small amount of soot buildup will noticeably increase your baking time.

Nessmuk didn't bother with any of this, however. To do it his way, either wrap a thick ribbon of bannock dough around a green stick or wrap your dough in leaves. Exercise care in selecting the stick or leaves, avoiding strong tasting (such as evergreen) or toxic plant materials.

The following recipes can be produced in the frying pan, Dutch oven, or reflector. Each will give you about one "batch," or as much as will comfortably bake at once.

Some of the recipes are based on a basic bannock mix which is added to, or in some cases sightly adjusted, to make different doughs. The backpacker or lightweight canoe camper can really utilize bannock to the fullest, carrying just the basic mix and altering and adding to it from his stores.

Breads

For starters, just to get your technique down, try this.

Johnnycake

1 quart cornmeal
1 pint hot water
$1/4$ teaspoon salt

Mix the ingredients, form them into a flat cake, and bake in frying pan, Dutch oven, or reflector oven.

Basic Bannock Mix

1 cup flour
1 teaspoon baking powder
$1/4$ teaspoon salt
$1/4$ cup dry milk powder
1 tablespoon shortening

Sift the dry ingredients, then mix in the shortening until the whole mixture is granular like course sand, and package it in large, heavy-duty plastic bags.

The basic bannock mix will be the foundation of your baking powder recipes. Mixing up a bannock or cornbread in camp without making a mess of major proportions can be accomplished in several ways. The most common is to add water, or milk if you have it, to the bag (package your dry bannock mix in oversized heavy gauge plastic bags for this reason) containing the dry mix, and knead this briefly. Another way is to use a flat surface, such as an overturned canoe or the top of your camp kitchen, as a mixing board.

I like to find some kind of a bowl, then place the dry mix in it and add water, stirring with a stick or spoon until it clings. This leaves no mess on hands or equipment and saves time. Water meeting baking powder is what causes the carbon dioxide that raises the bread to form. The quicker you get the dough from the mixing bowl to your preheated, oiled pan or oven the better it will turn out.

Bannock mix can be prepackaged for convenience.

Real cornbread is a long way from Johnnycake. This recipe can be bagged up ahead of time like the bannock. Cornbreads keep well. Make up an extra portion and take it along for lunch while traveling the next day.

Cornbread

1 cup cornmeal
$1/2$ cup flour
$1/4$ teaspoon salt
2 teaspoons baking powder
1 tablespoon dry milk
2 tablespoon shortening
1 egg (optional)
Water

Sift the dry ingredients and work in the shortening until the mixture is granular. Add 1/3 to 1/2 cup water and an egg, if you have one in camp. Form the mixture into a flat loaf and bake it in an oiled Dutch oven, reflector, or frying pan.

Pancakes

No matter what Nessmuk thought about flapjacks, I'll be surprised if anyone ever turns them down in my camp. For syrup, there is a maple-flavored concentrate available from the grocery store, or syrup crystals obtainable from freeze-dried foods suppliers for campers who travel light, or brown sugar or jam will do just fine.

Bannock Pancakes

To a bag of basic bannock mix add:
$1/4$ cup sugar
1 egg if you have it
Enough water to make a batter

Beat just enough to mix and no more, a few lumps are okay. Oil your frying pan with bacon fat if you have some in camp.

Here is something you can feed your camp that they probably don't get at home:

Corn Pancakes

2 cups cornmeal
1 cup flour
1 tablespoon baking powder
1 tablespoon sugar
$1/4$ tablespoon salt
3 tablespoons dry milk
1 egg
Water

Mix the dry ingredients, add an egg, then add enough water to make a stiff batter. Pour onto heated, oiled frying pan or Dutch oven lid.

The dry ingredients in this recipe can also be prepared ahead of time. As in the bannock cakes, the egg is optional.

If you want to give sourdough a try, do it either during warm weather or in a tent or cabin with a constant heat supply. There really aren't many things in the world better than sourdough pancakes, and some of the bother can be avoided by pre-packaging the dry ingredients as you do your bannock mix.

Most sourdough bakers like to work with a starter, which is a pre-made yeast culture. This recipe starts from "scratch" for the sake of simplicity. Using a starter is a better way to go if you will be making sourdough on a regular basis, either in camp or at home, but a starter needs some special care and management. There are many fine books on baking, some that deal exclusively with sourdough, that contain a complete explanation of sourdough starters.

Adam's County Sourdough Pancakes

You will need two bags:

Bag #1

1 $1/2$ cups whole wheat flour
1 $1/2$ cups white flour
1 envelope yeast

Bag #2

$1/2$ teaspoon salt

2 tablespoons brown sugar

1 teaspoon baking soda

2 tablespoons shortening

3 tablespoons dry milk

Work the shortening in the second bag into the dry ingredients as you did for the bannock mix. The night before your pancake breakfast, put Bag #1 and three cups of warm water in a bowl. This needs a warm place to sit overnight for the yeast culture to grow, which can be a problem in some camps under some conditions. If your overnight temperature was agreeable, you will have a strong-smelling bubbling mixture called a sponge awaiting you in the morning. Add Bag #2 to this, along with an egg if you have it, and more water if needed to make a batter of proper pancake consistency. Cook as you would any other pancakes.

Biscuits and Dumplings

These are variations of your basic bannock recipe. You can either roll out the bannock dough and cut biscuits like cookies before they go on the heat, or add more water and make drop biscuits. You can get by with a good iron frying plan with a lid but the Dutch or reflector oven is needed to do a really nice job.

Biscuits can be either the rolled and cut type or the drop biscuit variety.

The same can be done in the morning with the bannock, or better yet, your corn pancake mix. Use the reflector or Dutch oven and have some jam or jelly on hand.

Those stews that are a bit short on an ingredient or two can be saved with a few dumplings or by topping the dish with bannock mix the consistency of the drop biscuits. Wait until the stew is cooked, then add the dough or dumplings, pile fresh coals from the fire on the lid, and wait ten minutes before checking the contents.

Baked Desserts

The evening meal is often the time for getting elaborate. Camping in the fall, in particular, with the weather cold enough to build up an appetite but not enough to drive everyone off to bed early, is the time to turn out some high calorie after-dinner treats.

A bannock "coffee cake" makes a fine dessert, and the leftovers (or make an extra) are just the ticket for breakfast the next morning.

Camp Coffee Cake

1 cup flour
2 teaspoons baking powder
$1/4$ teaspoon salt
$1/2$ cup instant hot chocolate mix
$1/2$ cup sugar
2 tablespoons shortening
$1/4$ cup dry milk
Water

Bag up the dry ingredients ahead of time. Add water and bake as you would the cornbread.

Top your coffee cake with marmalade, jam, or to improvise in the field mix together some more chocolate beverage powder, sugar, water, and dry milk or coffee creamer for a frosting.

Fruit Pies and Tarts

You already have the necessary ingredients, except for the fruit, with your food stores. Use bannock mix, or better yet use your coffee cake mixture. Add less water. Roll it out to make a dough.

At this point you can use a greased pie tin and line it with the dough, add whatever you have in the way of fruit for filling, and cover it with the remaining dough, punching a few slits in it to allow steam to escape.

A tart is put together in almost the same way, simply eliminating the pie tin and crimping the dough together where the sides meet with a fork and a little water.

Seal the edges of the tart with a fork and a little water.

Canned pie fillings are the easiest to work with, but the weight conscious or traditionalist outdoor baker can do very well with dried fruits. Soak dried apricots, apples, peaches, or whatever overnight, and cook the fruit in its water with some brown sugar to thicken before adding it to the pastry shell. Add a couple tablespoons of cold water with a pinch of cornstarch to the boiling fruit and water if any additional thickening is needed.

one six- or eight-ounce bag of dried fruit per batch or bannock dough will be about right.

Bake your treats as you would a bannock in either the reflector or Dutch oven. Your temperature will have to be right on for these as they are thicker and have the partially liquid filling. Not too hot, or you'll have a cold interior, not too cold, or the dough won't firm up and hold together.

8

Outdoor Ovens

If the chain of circumstances that led to this book has any definite root, it's a cast iron frying pan smoking over the fire pit of a Wisconsin deer camp more than a decade ago. Cooking techniques involving any utensil other than that pan and a few others like it were foreign to that camp. The dominating presence of fried potatoes and onions, fried eggs, fried pancakes, fried bannock, fried ham, and a handful of fried onions to grace whatever meat was cooked was replacing the anticipation of fine outdoor meals with the gag reflex.

Dutch ovens—Get a Real One

The Dutch oven is the closest you can get to a universal camp cooking utensil. Most any recipe for most any food, with the exception of broiling on a grate, can be adapted to it. Small amounts of game, one or two grouse or woodcock, for example, can be stretched with a game stew or added to a hearty vegetable soup to supply dinner for three or four.

The first sensible step away from the frying pan is an oven. In our case the first was a Dutch oven, and the problem was finding one. No one's great-aunt had one kicking around in the attic, and neither the local sporting goods store nor the hardware store were of any help. Looking in the catalogs of mail order sporting goods dealers paid off, and after parting with about thirty-five dollars we were in business.

Along the way I ran into various cooking utensils that were billed as Dutch ovens—pots made of aluminum or steel, or with flat bottoms

134

instead of the characteristic legs of a true Dutch oven. If you're going to do a decent job of cooking outdoors in a Dutch oven you will need the real thing. Purchase only cast iron because of its superior heat retention, consistency of surface temperature, and non-stick cooking surface. Make sure that it has the three stubby legs to hold it from direct heat and the lip around the edge of the lid to prevent ashes from falling into the pot when the lid is removed. Be careful with it. Don't be fooled by the heavy metal and massive construction—cast iron is very brittle, and dropping either oven or lid will likely result in a costly welding job.

*A real Dutch oven has legs, a protective rim around the lid,
and is made of cast iron.*

Breaking in a New Dutch Oven

Teflon and its offspring have allowed many of us to grow up without experiencing the best non-stick cooking surface of all: properly treated cast iron. New Dutch ovens need to be thoroughly scrubbed with a strong detergent to remove the anti-rust coating applied at the factory, and then "seasoned," or "sweetened" (depending on which part of the country you hail from), by rubbing the inside surface of the oven and lid with cooking oil and baking it in an oven at 300° F or so for four or five hours. This process opens the pores of the cast iron, filling them with the oil, which develops the non-stick cooking surface. If you do your part by not seriously burning any food to it, cleaning it by just rinsing and wiping the inside without any detergent other than a mild dishwashing soap, and oiling it lightly and faithfully after each use, it will serve you well and do a better job than any space-age coating.

Designing a Fire for Dutch Oven Cooking

The outstanding quality of the Dutch oven is its ability to supply a constant, even heat without "hot spots" that will burn the contents. This slow heat transfer takes some getting used to. Remember that the oven has to be preheated long enough to bring the metal up to cooking temperature before placing any food in it. Placing more coals on the lid of the oven than directly underneath it will result in more evenly cooked foods and less chance of burning as there is an air space between the metal surface and the food within. This is the reason for the legs of a true Dutch oven. While they may not completely suspend the oven over the fire surface, they will keep the weight of the oven from pressing down directly on the coals so an excessively hot cooking surface is not created.

Your Dutch oven will work best if your campfire is designed around it. Gather enough rocks to line the hole that will contain the oven to form a reflective, heat-retaining well. Avoid those from stream beds or wet areas as they absorb enough water to cause them to sometimes explode when heated. once the wall of the fire pit and the metal of the oven is preheated, it's almost impossible to overcook a meal with this even, gentle heat source.

Techniques for Dutch Oven Pit Baking

The Dutch oven leads naturally to pit baking. Leaving the oven in a hole in the ground packed with plenty of hot coals allows the work of cooking to go on while the cook is away fishing. While the basic idea is simple enough, there are a few rules that have to be followed to end up with an edible product.

Our first attempt with the pit cooking standby, baked beans, produced a rather interesting substance resembling a mixture of gravel, coffee grounds, and river-bottom mud. It was undercooked from not getting the oven heated up properly first. Dig your hole larger than you

The first step for using a pit oven is starting a fire over it.

think you will need, because you will want plenty of space for coals around the Dutch oven. Either build a good-sized fire over the top of the pit, interspersed with rocks to hold the heat, or line the bottom of the pit and as far up the sides as you can with rocks and get a real blaze going in the bottom. The rocks and surrounding earth have got to be dry and heated or the heat will be absorbed when you bury the pot, leaving little heat for cooking.

Place the Dutch oven in the pit on a layer of hot coals, cover the lid and sides with more coals, and cover the pit with green leaves, wet burlap, aluminum foil, or some other non-flammable material, and then a thin layer of earth. Don't pile on the damp clay like we did the first time and put the fire out. Digging out your pit cooked meal when you figure it's ready demands caution so as not to dislodge the lid. When done with the pit, do a thorough job of dousing the fire.

The safety aspects of cooking in a pit oven center around whether the pit can be left unattended. The weather, ground moisture, soil type

*Foil makes a good pit oven cover to keep soil
from laying directly on the coals.*

and other factors all figure in the prevalence of any safety hazard. They help determine whether you want to leave your supper to cook itself or if you should remain in or near camp. Watch out for tree roots—they can smolder and spread fire underground, starting a fire away from your pit hours or days afterward.

Cover the Dutch oven when pit cooking with foil or wet burlap, and use dry soil to cover the pit.

A Bean Recipe for Dutch Oven Beginners

I mentioned earlier that my first attempt with cooking beans in the pit met with disaster. Subsequent bean attempts, however, were well worth the effort come supper time. The pit cooking technique does require a bit of trial and error to master, so I recommend a bean recipe for beginners if only for the fact that if you mess up the first attempt or so it won't set your wallet back a noticeable amount.

Pit-cooked Baked Beans

1 quart navy beans
$1/2$ lb. bacon
1 large onion, sliced
1 teaspoons salt
1 tablespoon molasses
1 tablespoon brown sugar
1 teaspoon dry mustard

Soak the beans overnight and drain them before using. Lay half the bacon on the bottom of the Dutch oven, add the rest of the ingredients, stir, and lay the rest of the bacon across the top. Bake all day in your pit oven.

Remove the Dutch oven carefully from the pit to avoid jarring the lid.

Bobotie—A South African Pioneer Favorite

This recipe is South African in origin, but it's a true pioneers' dish. It was invented by the Dutchmen who opened up the frontier to white settlement in that country in the last century. This dish is a bit different than most camp chow you will find in this country, but is very good. Bobotie is a fine way to use game meats. Give it a try in the Dutch oven.

Bobotie

2 lbs finely chopped meat

2 tablespoons butter or margarine

1 cup milk

1 large onion, chopped fine

2 tablespoons curry powder

1 tablespoon brown sugar

1 teaspoon salt

$1/2$ teaspoon black pepper

$1/4$ cup lemon juice

3 eggs

4 bay leaves

2 slices bread

Brown the meat and onion in butter or margarine in a Dutch oven. Soak the bread in the milk. When the meat is browned add curry powder, brown sugar, pepper, salt, and lemon juice. Stir and allow this to warm up while you squeeze the milk from the bread. Then add the bread to the oven, and reserve the milk. Stir the contents of the oven again and tuck in the bay leaves. Beat the eggs into the milk, pour over the top of the other ingredients in the oven, and bake in the fire pit.

Reflector Oven—A Lightweight Alternative

The first portage on one of my canoe trips to the Boundary Waters Canoe Area Wilderness in northern Minnesota went okay, but by the end of the second portage I was questioning my judgment regarding the weight of the duffel bag balanced on my shoulders. The third, and longest, portage was a good three-quarters of a mile of stumbling over rocks and storm-felled trees that left me drenched with sweat and limping from a fall taken halfway along, the fall accelerated by the duffel bag with its eighteen-pound Dutch oven which imbedded itself in my back. I really liked cooking in the Dutch oven, but I didn't like it that much. Next trip, it was replaced with a reflector oven.

It almost wasn't, however. The reflector oven has been buried deep beneath the onslaught of convenience camping foods, even deeper than the Dutch oven, and it was only after an extensive search that I located two mail-order sporting goods suppliers and one store in a major metropolitan area that carried this item. They're old favorites in canoe country, with the emphasis on "old." These days, the backwoods canoe tripper is handed a pack of freeze dried entrees and a camp stove and he's on his way. He's still in some of the most beautiful and unpopulated country in North America, but without much of a menu to enjoy along the way.

The reflector oven folds flat, and its one or two pounds of weight make it a breeze to portage and acceptable for shorter backpacking trips. It does have some peculiarities that make it tricky for the beginner, however.

Using Radiant Heat with a Reflector oven

The reflector makes use of radiant heat, doing without a direct heat source to the utensil used in it. The glowing coals used for any other kind of outdoor cooking aren't much help here. You need a real blaze to transfer enough heat. That's just the ticket in much of the northern and western United States where most firewood will be fast-burning evergreens which make inferior coals for grilling or broiling.

Once your fire is burning well make sure that you have plenty of fuel on hand to maintain the temperature. Keep the fire as hot as is practical, adjusting the heat by moving the oven. Learning to control the heat takes some time and practice, more than handling the Dutch oven. Practice with the reflector at home in front of the fireplace or in the yard before you have to count on your skill with it to produce a meal in camp.

The reflector oven utilizes direct heat—a very hot fire will be necessary.

The limited capacity of the reflector oven probably restricts it from providing baked goods for a larger camp, but it is ideal for the backpacking or canoeing duo. Trout with mint leaves, or a brace of grouse or teal stuffed with cranberries, are a couple of possibilities if you put your gathering skills to work along with those of the hunter. Reflector cooking is generally drier than the Dutch oven, so keep butter or other liquid handy for basting, or cover or wrap the game. The front of the oven—towards the fire—can be hotter or cooler than the back depending on the angle at which the oven faces the fire, the heat of the fire, and the wind, so periodically rotate the food in order to cook it evenly.

Even with their limted capacity, reflectors are versatile, and many foods can be cooked in them if conditions allow for a large fire.

The Coleman camp oven fits neatly on top of their gasoline stove.

The Coleman Camp oven

The Coleman camp oven fits neatly on top of any of the countless green two and three burner stoves kicking around in garages across the country, offering a means of baking and roasting in camp during periods of no rain (when the Forest Service or other entities ban open fires) and during periods of too much rain when a roaring campfire or bed of glowing coals is little more than a soggy memory.

The oven unfolds from a flat, easily stowed package into enough space for two teal, a venison roast for two, or a small pan of biscuits. The thermometer on the door eliminates having to guess the oven temperature.

9

Over the Open Fire

I'll admit it—the first time I put a whole duck on the grill I wasn't convinced it was a good idea. Forces beyond my control, mainly an attack of mal de roasting pan brought on by too many waterfowl and venison dinners appearing from behind the oven door, drove me from the kitchen outside onto the porch. Cleaning the freezer had brought the tag ends of last season's game inventory to light. Two mallards.

It worked so well it was the featured recipe in camp on the opening day of the duck season that year—fat, corn-fed mallards sharing the grate with a teal and a wood duck. What had been a mere convenience and change of pace at home that spring became the favored method of providing a duck dinner in camp without going to the time and effort of roasting.

Broiling on the Grate

Don't get me wrong. I'm a big fan of the Dutch oven and reflector oven, but I do much of my camp cooking, and a lot of my better work, at that, either broiling directly on a grate or frying in a cast iron pan over the open fire.

The original camp cooking method was broiling. Sort of. Heaving an animal into the fire, dragging it out later on, scraping off the ashes, and dining alfresco with little ceremony has changed little in the parts of the world where it is still practiced, except now the knives are made of metal instead of stone. South American cowboys, to name one group, still use this time-honored method. By expanding our over-the-

*The majority of fire pits supllied by the Forest Service in
their campgrounds are unsuitable for cooking.*

fire cooking skills away past the time-honored heave and scrape stage
we can produce some really fine meals without the tough, dried out,
shoe-leather reputation that grilling game over flames has earned.
With a little knowledge, fish, venison, game birds, small game, and
even vegetables can come off the grill in fine form and with little effort.

It's unfortunate, but many of the cooking facilities provided in state
and national campgrounds are grossly inadequate. They require large
fires which are difficult to control and adjust, and the fireplaces provided don't hold the grates packed by typical campers.

The only way to cook over the fire with this Sate Forest grate is with a blazing fire, large enough to reach the height of the concrete blocks.

Cooking over the fire allows the camper to travel light, whether the utensils be carried on his back, canoe, horse, or vehicle. The backpacker or canoe tripper needs only a pack, a lightweight folding grate, and a steel or cast-iron frying pan to be fully equipped.

There are those who would shudder at the sight of a frying pan, however, and with good reason. Camp cooks earlier in the century would leave for the woods with a frying pan, a chunk of bacon or salt pork, some dry beans, and flour and baking powder for making bannock. Fish taken along the way would usually end up in the frying pan as well as any slow animal. Though some of these woodsmen adapted well to this monotonous, tiresome diet, the average camper, then as now, would be unable to look a frying pan in the eye for quite some time after a week in the woods.

It doesn't have to be that way. By using the fire and grate in some different ways we can retain the light weight, minimum bulk, short cooking times, and simple technique without having to resort to the bannock and beans diet.

This steel fire pit is better than most, but the camp cook still must build too large of a fire to make it work.

Cooking Ribs in Camp

Camp cooks have some very hard-and-fast opinions about game ribs. They're either just the finest game-meat meal imaginable, or they taste so gamey that they go into the bone bucket with the scrap at butchering time. No animal ribs, even beef, have a lot of meat compared to the other cuts. Big-game animals are sparser yet. In addition, ribs carry layers of fat between the meat. In the case of venison or other game, the ribs may carry that strong, gamey flavor that most folks find objectionable. Ribs cooked in a pan, oven, or crock pot are usually responsible for this complaint. Cooking directly over the heat source, which allows the ribs to drain their fat while they cook, draws off much of the gamey taste and leaves one of the really fine game dishes for the few that know the secret.

*You can avoid the weight of the cast iron
frying pan using a steel saute pan.*

One way of cooking ribs in camp is to take two whole racks and cut down between the bones for a couple inches along the side of the rack away from the spine. Then lean them over the fire in an "A" frame shape, with the cut ends of the ribs interleaved like the fingers of folded hands to hold them together. An easier method, that allows the ribs to cook more evenly and is easier to control, is just to lay the rack on the grill. Small grills can be accommodated by cutting the rack of ribs down the center through the bones perpendicularly, with an ax, hatchet, or large knife.

Salt, pepper, a little garlic, and some onion powder are all that is needed to ready them for the fire. Season both sides. You'll have to be conscious of the heat level of the cooking fires. There's not a whole lot of meat on game ribs, and too much heat will leave you with a charred, dried-out mess in which the bone is indistinguishable from the meat.

A better method is to marinade the ribs and baste them with a barbecue sauce, using the rib marinade in the Sauces and Marinades chapter. Let them soak in this mixture overnight, and place them directly onto the grill over a bed of hot coals. You will want about a medium heat, with no flames.

Let the ribs warm through and start to cook on the outside. Then swab on the barbecue sauce, using either a bottled variety or the recipe in the Sauces and Marinades chapter. After that is on, cook the ribs until done. Ribs take longer than you would think—the muscle tissue along those bones is stringy and demands a long, slow cooking time. Restaurants that serve beef or pork ribs either boil, steam, or roast them ahead of time for this reason.

Test them for doneness by trying to separate the bones with a fork or knife. When they pull away easily from one another, they are done.

Venison Steaks

Steaks are a natural for the open fire and grate. We usually eat up the last of the previous season's venison on the first fishing and camping trip of the spring. The absolutely finest way to enjoy a venison steak is to take the hind legs to a butcher, and have them cut into round steaks. Tell the meat cutter that you'll be cooking them on the grill so he doesn't cut them too thick. The resulting steaks will look just like the round steaks you see wrapped in plastic at the meat counter, bone and all. You can use the venison marinade or the universal marinade in the Sauces and Marinades chapter, or your venison steaks will be fine with just a dusting of salt, pepper, and garlic powder unless the deer was an older animal or didn't receive top-quality field care after it was killed.

Rabbits and Squirrels

Rabbit and squirrel don't do well over the open fire. The fat that is scarce in any small game is nonexistent in these two—they are just too dry to broil. The frying pan, however, does a fine job. older animals should be parboiled first.

Fried Rabbit or Squirrel

1 rabbit or squirrel
1 onion, sliced
Seasoned flour
1 egg
1 cup milk
Cracker or bread crumbs

Cut the rabbit or squirrel into eating-size pieces. If the rabbit is particularly large or old, parboil first. Beat the egg and mix it with the milk. Dip the pieces into the seasoned flour, then into the egg and milk mixture, and then into the cracker crumbs, coating them. Fry it in the cast iron skillet in hot oil, add the onions when half done, and cover the pan to finish cooking. Make pan gravy according to instructions in the *Sauces and Marinades* chapter.

Stuffed Fish

The spot where we camp in the national forest during the deer season is along a trail used by other hunters walking to their stands. Since camping in the snow is not as popular now as it once was in these parts, we've become something of a minor tourist attraction, with members of hunting parties on their way through stopping to say hello.

By far the strongest reaction we've gotten out of any of these guys was the afternoon we came in a little early from the woods. We had the lake trout stuffed and laid on the grate over the fire. You would think some of those guys had never seen a fish in their life, but on further thought. they'd probably never see again a camp with a twenty-five inch, stuffed and trussed lake trout slowly broiling on a grate.

The trout was the product of another expedition earlier in the year, of course, and had spent part of the summer and fall patiently waiting in my home freezer. The stuffing was made like this.

Stuffing for Fish
5 cups bread crumbs or diced dry bread
1 small onion
$1/2$ stalk celery
$1/2$ dozen mushrooms
4 tablespoons butter
2 eggs
Salt
Granulated garlic
Lemon juice or 1 lemon
Water

Dice the celery, mushrooms, and onion and lightly fry them in the butter. Add the bread crumbs or bread, a dash of salt and granulated garlic, a squirt of lemon juice or half the juice of the lemon, and two eggs. Mix, and add water until you have the consistency of stuffing.

If you have a few crayfish add the cooked tails to the above stuffing for a really nice accent. Fill the trout or salmon with the stuffing. You can sew the cavity shut with twine if you feel the need, or just be careful with it on the grill if you don't want to go to the trouble. It's a lot easier to cook trussed.

Melt a pound of butter and add some lemon juice to it. Use this to baste the fish while it is on the grill. oil the grill first to keep it from sticking.

Then get ready to enjoy one of the finest outdoor meals that will come your way. Feel good about it, you deserve it.

Smaller fish can also benefit from being cooked directly on the grate. Again, oil the grate to keep the fish from sticking and baste the fish as it cooks. Large, firm fillets, from a salmon, for instance, can be cooked on the grill if you are careful turning them over. Fish steaks are made for grilling, and any fish destined for the open fire that is large enough to get away with it should be dressed in this manner.

Ducks

If you're like me you've lost count of duck dinners you enjoyed which were roasted in ovens and Dutch ovens, baked in casseroles, stuffed with kraut or sausage or wrapped in bacon or foil. Most likely they were roasted in one way or another. And no matter how skilled you are at cooking, no matter how patiently your long-suffering summer palate has yearned for the opening of the season, you're going to tire of roasted birds sooner or later. With each year, it gets sooner.

Prepare a dressed duck for the grill by splitting it up the breast and flattening it. You may have to break some of the ribs by the backbone to allow it to lay flat. Lean on it with the flat of your hand.

Use the bird marinade in the Sauces and Marinades chapter. Give it three or four hours, or overnight if you have a fish-eating duck. Fish-eaters should be skinned, but the other species will do better if plucked. You will need moderate heat, like you had for the venison ribs. You're not cooking an inch-thick steak here.

A variation is to use a barbecue sauce. Any bottled or homemade sauce will do a fine job, but the ultimate barbecued duck is with a Chinese barbecue mixture called hoisin sauce.

Hoisin sauce is best described as a cross between a regular barbecue sauce and a sweet-and-sour sauce. It will give a bird a tart, tangy sweet-and-sour taste that will have you crunching the bones between your teeth. Hoisin sauce is inexpensive and can be found in the ethnic or oriental foods section of most grocery stores. It is definitely one of the better things you can do to a duck in camp. Do yourself a favor and try it.

Other game birds perform equally well on the grate. Pheasant is particularly good this way and the grate is a fine way to use the occasional grouse that shows up in camp during a deer hunt. Try to cover the bird with a lid to retain some of the smoke flavor.

Grilling Vegetables

You can complement your grilled game meats with vegetables, cooking them right on the grill alongside the entree. The classic, of course, is sweet corn. You can lay it on the grill just as it comes off the stalk, in the husk, or soak the cobs in water for an hour before putting them on the grill. This will steam the corn right in the husk as it cooks on the grill. We like it better like this.

The tassels can be removed either before cooking or as you husk them after they are cooked. Stopping at roadside stands on the way to camp provides corn that may have been picked that day. That's a real treat—even twenty-four hours between stalk and plate can make a big difference.

The common potato is often featured in camp. It travels well in winter and summer, is easily roasted around the fire, and if you live in potato-growing country the spuds are, quite literally, cheaper than rocks. The traditional method for cooking potatoes is the heave-and-scrape method mentioned earlier. Potatoes can go right into the coals, be buried under them, placed off to one side in the bottom of the fire pit, or put up on top on the grate. Turn them a lot.

Put the rest of your vegetables on the grill. Large onions can be peeled and cut in half, with the ends left intact to keep them from falling apart. Carrots usually are cut in half lengthwise. Lay mushrooms right on the grill or use a skewer. Try marinading them in the "universal marinade," separating Italian salad dressing, before you leave for camp, and baste them with that mixture as they broil, taking care to avoid coating them with smoke from the burning oil. By far the best vegetable cooked this way is the green pepper. Cut the peppers in half, remove the seeds and stems, marinate them, and broil them over the coals.

10

The Wok

China is a country which traditionally has had a lot of people to feed and not much meat to offer them. Sort of like some deer camps I've been in. A full meat pole, game bag, or stringer is nice, but certainly doesn't occur in any camp with enough regularity to plan meals around. This is where Chinese cuisine, the product of a fuel and meat-poor culture, really shines.

The Advantage of Stir-Fry Cooking

Creating stir-fry dishes in camp satisfies several demands of the practical camp cook. First you can get by—and do so very well indeed because the entire cuisine is designed this way—with relatively little meat as compared to traditional Western cooking.

Secondly, stir-fry cooking is simple. It requires minimal utensils and can be prepared as well over an open fire ten watery miles from the nearest highway as it can in a fully-equipped home kitchen. Stirfry cooking is peasant cooking, and guess what Chinese peasants used to cook over? You guessed it, an open fire.

Stir-frying generally requires less fuel than many camp cooking techniques. This can be an important factor under some conditions. You need an intense heat to get the wok hot and keep it that way throughout the cooking process, but there is no need for the lengthy, wood-consuming wait as your fire burns down to a bed of coals. Nor will you have to endure the long, gas-gulping simmering asked of a camp stove. Some stoves on the market have only one heat setting, conservatively described as inferno, or perhaps Mt. St.

Helens. This fearsome blast of unregulated heat that blackens ban-
nocks and burns the bottoms out of aluminum pots is just the ticket for
stir-frying where hotter is better.

The natural flavors and colors of foods are enhanced and intensi-
fied when they are stir-fried. The quick application of heat neither dulls
the brilliant colors of vegetables nor destroys the vitamin content.
Meats are not overcooked, but cooked until just done, with similar
nutritional benefit.

A final stir-frying benefit is built into the cuisine itself. A stir-fried
meal enables the camp cook to stretch a duck or a lonely brace of
grouse or a dozen crayfish to feed three, four, or five campers.

Finally, stir-frying is fast. Hot, great-tasting, nutritious camp meals
can be whipped out in a wok in literally half the time you would spend
on a similar repast using some Western cooking method. You can be
sitting down to a gourmet outdoor meal within an hour of first walking
or paddling into camp. You won't even have to wait for the fire to burn
down to coals as this technique demands a hot, reflector oven-type
fire.

Stir-frying is traditionally done in a wok, a cooking pan shaped like
half a sphere, from the size of a basketball on up to the giant institutional models. While stir-frying can be done in almost any pan, as long
as it is steel or cast iron for the heat-retention properties of these metals, the wok is easier to work. Its high sides prevent the contents from
spilling as you swirl them about, and the rounded, upward-sloping outside surface provides a more even heating surface. There are aluminum and thin lightweight steel woks on the market. These utensils
suffer from the same problems as similarly constructed frying pans.
They tend to form "hot spots" directly at the point where the heat is
applied, conducting little of the energy to the rest of the cooking surface.

Seasoning a New Wok

The steel wok is seasoned much like the Dutch oven. Coat the
inside with a good, high-temperature oil such as peanut oil. Heat the
pan until the oil smokes, then allow it to cool. Wipe the inside thoroughly and repeat the process. While the ideal is to be a good cook

The wok was designed for use over an open fire.

and never burn any food to the surface of your wok, requiringonly a gentle wipe to clean it after use, reality sometimes deigns otherwise.

Wash your wok with a mild soap only. Stay away from any kind of grease cutter -type of chemicals, and oil and heat it again after each use. This is less of a job than it seems from reading about it. Simply give the inside of the wok a quick wipe with the oil and set it over the fire or stove as you conduct some other after-dinner chore. The cooking surface of your wok will turn black with use. Your scrubbing instincts will rebel against this. Resist. This is the original non-stick cooking surface, and it will serve you well if you take care of it.

Stir-frying requires cooking oil. While any old oil, strictly speaking, will work, try to stay away from the generic salad or cooking oils. Peanut oil is the best bet for stir-frying. It has a good flavor, it's okay

for any other oil usage in camp, and it can handle the high temperatures found both in wok cooking and in seasoning the wok, Dutch
oven, or iron frying pan without burning.

Stir-frying as a method of cooking is different from anything you
have taken on before. The idea is to apply intense heat to the food for
a very brief period. It really is about as easy as that, and the technique
offers several unique benefits.

The Technique of Stir-Frying

Before we cook from a recipe, let's run through the technique of
stir-frying. You must have all the necessary ingredients laid out, ready
to go and handy to reach, before you begin. The in-and-out-of-the-
pan style of cooking here leaves no room for fumbling around through a
pack or field kitchen searching for ingredients, and setting the meal
aside halfway through will definitely not add to a meal that is designed
to be cooked quickly and served hot.

Cut your vegetables long and thin, when possible, avoiding the
small, diced style of Western cooking. If using cuts of meat (as
opposed to quartering a bird or smaller animal), cut the slices thin,
long, and against the grain. The faster each piece of meat or vegetable
cooks, the better it will taste in your stir-fried meal.

First, prepare your fire or stove and fuel it so it's hot and will stay
that way through the ten or fifteen minutes you'll spend cooking. If
you'll be serving rice with the meal (a natural, nutritious, and tasty
accompaniment), cook it ahead of time and set the pot by the fire to
stay warm—stir-frying will require all your attention.

Once your wok is hot almost to the point of making the oil smoke,
add some or all of the food ingredients. Stir-frying demands that the
high temperature stay pretty constant throughout the process, hot
enough to make the meat or vegetables crackle. If you're making any
more than a very small recipe, then begin with the meats and cook the
ingredients one or two at a time.

There's the frying, now for the stirring. The food ingredients must
be kept in constant motion, stirring while they cook. The moment you
let them lay against the sides or bottom of the wok with all that intense
heat for more than a moment you are going to overcook something.
You want meats cooked just through, at most, and vegetables left with

most of their bright colors. They should still be almost as crunchy as when they entered the wok. There are various impressive oriental-looking cooking utensils on the market, but for our purposes a spatula or wooden spoon works very well and can serve for other camp kitchen chores as well.

The recipes we'll use here are bound with a liquid mixture of a stock, cornstarch, and soy sauce for seasoning. After the meats and vegetables have been cooked and set aside, heat the wok again and add the meats and vegetables and the stock all together. As this mixture heats up it will thicken. Remove the wok from the fire, and eat.

This process is so simple it doesn't take much more time to accomplish than it has taken you to read about it. It's also incredibly adaptable to changes in recipe items. Stir-frying a meal can absorb with ease and style any kind of meat or fish taken during the day, nuts gathered, and mushrooms or wild edible plants picked.

Here's a simple camp stir-fry recipe, a good one to begin with. You can bone the ducks if you want to take the time and trouble, I usually just quarter them. Cook the duck quarters first, as they will take considerably longer due to their large size.

Stir-fry Mallard

2 ducks (grouse, pheasant, etc.)
2 tablespoons peanut oil
2 carrots, sliced thin
1 large onion, sliced thin
2 cloves garlic, diced
2 stalks celery, sliced thin
1 cup chicken stock (made with bouillon cube)
4 teaspoons cornstarch
1/4 cup soy sauce
Cooked rice to go with the meal

Fry the garlic in the oil. When it's just cooked through, remove and discard it. Cook the duck or bird pieces until just cooked through, then remove. Add the vegetables to the wok, one at a time, removing as each is just warmed through. Add more peanut oil if needed. Mix the soy sauce, chicken stock, and cornstarch. Add to the wok, stirring first as the cornstarch tends to settle on the bottom, and when boiling, add the cooked ingredients you have previously set aside. When the liquid again comes to a boil and the sauce thickens, remove from the heat immediately.

The wok is a great way to cook strong-tasting fish-eating ducks. Skin and trim the fat from the birds. Marinate them overnight in a mixture of two parts water, two parts red or white wine, and one part soy sauce.

This stir-fry uses beef as the meat item. By substituting freeze-dried or dehydrated vegetables from an oriental grocery store for the fresh carrots and onions and dried mushrooms, it fits right into the backpacker or canoe camper's menu.

Beef Jerky Oriental

1 clove garlic
1 cup, or about 6 sticks, beef jerky
1/2 cup mushrooms, sliced
1 carrot, sliced thin
1 small onion, sliced thin
1/2 cups nuts, acorns if available
2 tablespoons peanut oil
1/4 cup water
1/4 cup soy sauce
2 tablespoons cornstarch

Soak the jerky the night before to soften it, and cut it into bite-sized pieces. Heat the wok, add the oil, cook the garlic and discard it. one at a time (or double up if the quantities are small), cook the beef, carrot, onion, and mushrooms, and remove all from the wok. Mix the water, cornstarch, and soy sauce, add it to the wok, and when it's hot put the other ingredients back in the wok, along with the nuts.

Fresh water lobsters are easy and fun to catch, but you can't always get enough for a crayfish boil. Prepare the crayfish by soaking them in fresh water to purge them, then boil them in salted water with a shot of lemon juice, if you have it in camp, until the shells turn red. Remove them and let them cool. Break the tails from the crayfish, and crack the shells to extract the meat. Reserve the cooking water.

Stir-fried Crayfish Tails

2 dozen crayfish tails
$1/2$ cup sliced fresh mushrooms
$1/2$ small onion, sliced thin
2 stalks celery, sliced thin
2 tablespoons peanut oil
1 teaspoon cornstarch
$1/4$ cup water from cooking crayfish
$1/4$ cup soy sauce
$1/4$ teaspoon cayenne pepper
1 small piece ginger root

Heat the oil in the wok and cook and discard the ginger root. Cook the mushrooms, celery, and onion and remove. Mix the water from boiling the crayfish, soy sauce, and cornstarch and add to the wok. When the mixture is boiling add the cooked vegetables and crayfish tails. Add cayenne pepper, using more than the $1/4$ teaspoon if you appreciate hot food.

For a really solid, hot dish, replace the cayenne pepper with some sliced jalapeno peppers, fried and discarded with the ginger root.

Don't Forget the Rice

I can't prove this, but I suspect that at least as much rice is cooked outdoors over open fires around the world each day as is cooked indoors in civilized kitchens. Around a third of the world's population eats rice every day. "Wilderness potatoes," as rice was named by trappers in the white silence of the north country in the last century, lends itself admirably to the camp kitchen. It is light, nutritious andwill not

spoil if kept reasonably dry. It is a good energy-provider for active outdoors people. It tastes great plain, and lends itself to an endless variety of rice dishes, from serving as a side dish or base to those mentioned in this chapter, to rice pudding for dessert.

Cooking rice is one of the greatest exercises in simplicity found in
either the civilized or wild kitchen. Use two parts water to one part rice.
Boil the water, add the rice, simmer for fifteen or twenty minutes.
That's all. Eat it.

Once you use your wok a few times I wager you'll take it along
more often. There are things it does not do well—the curved bottom is
not the answer for the fried egg, for example—but the backpacker or
canoe tripper willing to experiment a little might find the answer to the
ultimate, one pan-only trail kitchen to be one of the world's oldest
cooking utensils.

11

Sauce It

The history of sauces is incomplete at best. They're described in the literature of classical French cooking, which catalogs over two hundred individual sauces, as liquid seasonings. But their history goes further back, and is mired in the casual sanitary practices and primitive or nonexistent refrigeration of the Roman period and the Middle Ages in the Old World. Sauces originally were used more to cover the taste of meats approaching putrefaction than to enhance their natural flavors.

All too often in camp cooking, the sauce, or gravy if you prefer than term, hasn't progressed too many steps from its disreputable origins. Sauces in some cases are called upon to cover the taste or appearance of foods than have been improperly handled before ever reaching the grill or pot, such as fish or game that has not received proper care in the field, or wholesome raw materials that have been subjected to some form of abuse by the camp cook. For folks who just aren't too concerned with the quality of food they eat the answer to a burnt, raw, or otherwise ill-prepared and noxious meal is to smother it with some sort of sauce. out of sight, out of mind. But certainly not out of taste.

The ability to turn out a few simple sauces and make intelligent use of marinades will do as much for your camp cooking as several other skills combined. While we aren't going to shoot here for the ability to produce those two hundred sauces that we mentioned above, let's take a look at the basics.

The addition of a simple sauce can make the crowning touch on a camp meal.

Basic Sauce Components

A sauce is made up of three components: stock, seasoning and thickener. The stock is water flavored with any meat, fish, or vegetable, such as the liquid part of chicken soup. The seasoning can range from a simple shake of salt to entire bouquets of herbs. The thickener can be anything from a cooked mixture of flour and fat to a grated potato. The thickener is the most difficult for the novice camp cook to handle. There's no reason why an equal-quality product can't be turned out in a camp kitchen using a gasoline stove and utilizing an overturned canoe for a table as can be prepared in the most extensively equipped home kitchen. By the end of this chapter we'll be doing just that.

The first step to making this a pleasurable and good tasting addition to camp cooking is to keep it under control. Not every meal calls for a sauce or gravy. Sometimes one is simply not needed to complement that which perhaps better stands alone. In other situations time, inclement weather, or a tired cook cause a good sauce or gravy to be omitted. Saucing up a meal takes a little time and patience and is out of place in those meals that are meant to be merely belly-stuffers before collapsing into the sleeping bag.

Making Stock

The first item we'll discuss is stock. As we mentioned earlier this is no more, essentially, than flavored water. The issue is clouded, as usual, by the tradition and literature of cooking. The French win the prize with an intimidating list of ten basic stocks. Stock can be made from almost anything that is an animal or plant, but we will concern ourselves here mainly with chicken or beef stock. Either one or the other lends itself to almost any sauce recipe you will use. Both beef and chicken flavors are available as bases or the concentrated forms of stocks.

An exception occurs when roasting game meats in a Dutch oven or pan in a reflector oven. The easiest, and perhaps the best, stock is created simply by adding enough water to the roasting meat to form a stock in the pot as your meal cooks. With venison or other game you will want to remove the fat (which will likely be strong-tasting) from the stock. This is accomplished either by skimming it from the top of the hot liquid with a spoon or ladle or, if the stock is to be chilled and used later, the fat will rise to the surface and harden. It can then be easily removed by lifting it whole like a lid or scraping it from the top of the stock.

Sauces are best left for more leisurely dinners when
the cooks have time to concentrate on them.

You'll make little, if any, stock in camp. The process takes too long, plus constant heat is required which is not fitting with camp schedules unless you are roasting meat and making your stock right with it. But for the sake of knowing how to put it together, here's the basic idea. Game meats and bones need to be trimmed of fat in this case as in any other situation where you are cooking wild game.

Stock
Meat, bones, or trimmings of fish or game
Vegetables or vegetable scraps—carrot peelings,
     onion skins, celery tops, etc.
A few shakes of pepper
Simmer at a low boil overnight. Strain before using.

Not much to it. Little stock is made from scratch these days, however, even in restaurants. What we will use for our camp sauces, and what most of the sauces, gravies, and soups you have in homes and eating establishments these days are made from is soup base, which is no more than concentrated stock.

Stock Base
If you take a stock and boil it, and continue to boil it until you have no more than a paste or powder, you have what is known as a soup or stock base. Bases are simply combined with water to recreate the stock. They come in varieties that range from the normal chicken, beef, and pork, to such exotics as clam, lobster, and lamb. No one makes a venison base.

A simple guide to the quality of a base is to look at the ingredients label on the package. Federal Government labeling regulations specify that food ingredients must appear on the package in the order in which they proportionally appear in the product. A high quality beef base, for example, will list beef or beef fat first on the ingredients label, while a lower quality base will list salt first. Paying the price for the higher quality bases, those with meat as the first, or close to the first, ingredient is not only good culinary sense but good economic savvy as well. With the lower priced bases you are paying primarily for salt and food coloring.

Another gauge to the quality of a base is the amount of liquid present. Those bases with the consistency of a paste are at the top of the quality ladder. The amount of meat or fat in the bases steadily decreases along with the moisture as you go down the quality scale.

These varying quality levels of stock bases all have their place in the camp kitchen, however, and the form in which they're packed will influence some decisions. The standard bouillon cube is far from a quality base but the durable, space-saving packaging makes them a natural for the camp kitchen.

Sauce Thickeners

Thickeners for sauces range from a truly complicated system of mixing hot liquids and eggs know as a liaison (which has no place in a camp) to the simple whitewash—flour and water that is stirred into a boiling stock. For camp cooking and most home cooking you can restrict yourself to two different thickening methods and not miss a thing.

The first method uses a roux (pronounced "roo") as its primary ingredient. Roux is an equal mixture of flour and butter or any other fat which is slowly cooked over low heat until it just begins to change color. Roux is added to a hot stock in small quantities—perhaps a tablespoon at a time. As the stock continues to boil, and you continuously stir it with a fork or other utensil, it will begin to thicken. You can't rush it. Take your time and you will experience a smooth, velvety gravy.

Roux keeps well, so there's no reason to make it in camp. Cook it at home and store it in a suitable container for the type of camping you are doing. Margarine should be used if the weather will be warm, as butter will turn rancid with time.

Here are a couple of tips for using roux. First, make sure the mixture has the consistency of a paste, or is a little more liquid. The dryer and harder it is the more difficult it will be to get it to dissolve and thicken the sauce. Second, get it warm or hot before using. Cold roux takes its time dissolving and will cause lumps to form.

For example, one situation where a roux would be used in camp would be to thicken the liquid from roasting game or other meats in a Dutch oven. After removing the meat from the oven, taste the stock and add bouillon cubes or other bases or seasonings if you think it needs it. Bring the liquid back to a boil, and slowly add the roux, a little at a time, keeping the liquid boiling all the while. Too much roux can be corrected by adding more water or stock to thin the gravy.

The original camp and home cooking gravy is pan gravy, one version of which is quite similar to the gravy we outlined above. Here's how a camp cook can turn out a real treat of an outdoor meal using just a frying pan.

Fry grouse breasts, venison, rabbit, or any meat as you normally would. Use one of the recipes elsewhere in this book that calls for a cast iron frying pan or Dutch oven. Remove the meat when done, then loosen the cooked particles of meat from the bottom of the pan with a spatula or spoon. You are going to add flour to the frying fat already in the pan to make a roux. If there's not enough fat left after cooking the meat, add more butter or margarine.

After this roux in your pan has cooked for a moment, add milk (using dry milk if your transportation is feet or canoe) for a traditional-type pan gravy, or else water or stock. Allow this to boil, and add more roux if needed to thicken it further. You can season the gravy when thickened with bouillon cubes or some other base, or use salt, pepper, and other spices.

Thickening with cornstarch is mainly used in oriental cooking but will serve equally well in other situations. Cornstarch is light and compact, making it ideal for the backpacker and canoe cook. The mixture should be about one part cornstarch to three parts water. It must be stirred just before use as the cornstarch will settle to the bottom of the mixture in a very short time and stick there like cement.

The cornstarch and water mixture is added slowly to boiling stock. You can substitute some other liquid such as soy sauce for the water if you prefer it. Add the mixture slowly enough to maintain the boil and the stock will thicken. Cornstarch-thickened sauces acquire a shine and velvety texture that is quite different from sauces thickened with roux.

Basic Sauce Recipes

Along with the bases you'll need, the grocery store offers a large selection of instant sauces. While many of these are barely edible compared to what you can do yourself in camp, there are a few exceptions. Any product with the Knorr-Swiss label is worth looking into, particularly the Hollandaise sauce mix. There are others with which you may experiment. Lightweight trips can benefit greatly from some of these convenience products.

The first, most basic sauce for any cook is the white sauce. To modify it for a great fish sauce in camp, either replace half the milk with fish stock (perhaps some water in which you boiled a couple dozen crayfish), or add a little lemon juice and a sprinkling of parsley flakes or fresh parsley at the end.

White Sauce
4 tablespoons butter or margarine or bacon fat
4 tablespoons flour
2 cups milk
Salt and pepper

Make a roux with the flour and butter. After cooking long enough to heat it through (but not long enough to make it darken), add the milk. Continue heating until thickened.

As with any sauce, a too-thick mixture can be rescued by adding more liquid, and a too-thin mixture can be aided by adding more roux or cornstarch-and-water mixture.

A gravy for game birds, or chicken, is made like this:

Game Bird Gravy
4 tablespoons butter or other fat
4 tablespoons flour
2 cups chicken stock
Giblets from birds

Boil the giblets in the stock and remove them. Dice them when cool. Make a roux with the butter and flour, add the stock and stir until thickened. Add the diced cooked giblets.

Sauces for any other types of meats can be made using the same proportions of roux to liquid. If you're an expert mushroom forager, fresh picked mushrooms fried for just a moment in butter make an excellent addition to any sauce in camp. Use the butter then for the roux, saving it in another pan.

After you have created a few of the preceding recipes in camp, you may feel up to a challenge. one of the classic recipes in the line of sauces is Hollandaise. It is difficult to make properly, and also is difficult to keep warm without the sauce separating, but it's worth the effort.

One of the high culinary points of a recent hunting season was the evening that Mike (one of the ex-chefs that I camp and hunt with) created a Hollandaise sauce while squatting in the dirt by an open fire. Hollandaise, one of the classic sauces of French cooking, is a delightful addition to a camp meal, as much for the difficulty of producing it under primitive conditions and the sheer opulence of it as for the flavor of the sauce itself. Recipes always specify that the sauce be thickened over a double boiler with the water kept below the boiling point. The temperature of a Hollandaise as it thickens is critical. Stray just a tad above the boiling point and it separates and you're forced to start completely over.

This is advanced camp cooking, and I recommend that you master Hollandaise at home before attempting it afield. When you can make this sauce in the overturned steel lid of a camp cook kit over an open fire like Mike does, you know you've arrived as a camp cook.

Hollandaise Sauce

3 egg yolks
1 tablespoon cold water
$1/2$ cup butter or margarine
$1/8$ teaspoon lemon juice
A pinch of salt

Beat the egg yolks and water together with a fork. Heat this mixture in a double boiler, ensuring that the water in the bottom is not allowed to boil. Add the butter gradually, stirring the mixture as the sauce begins to thicken. After all the butter is used, add the lemon juice and salt. Thin it with warm water if necessary.

Hollandaise must be treated with equal care after the sauce is finished, making certain that it doesn't get any hotter than it was while cooking or it will separate.

This seems like a lot of time and trouble for one sauce, but Hollandaise complements a meal like little else. Just the sheer luxury of it in camp, gracing cattail shoots or wild asparagus, makes it more than worth the trouble.

Here is a good barbecue sauce for small game:

Barbecue Sauce

2 cups catsup
2 cups water
$1/2$ cup brown sugar
$1/4$ cup Worcestershire sauce
1 tablespoon celery salt
1 teaspoon pepper
1 large onion diced fine
$1/2$ teaspoon liquid smokeMix cold and refrigerate.

Try to make this up a week ahead of time so the flavors can mingle. Add more liquid smoke to the recipe if you like that smokey flavor, or eliminate it if the camp fire is enough for you.

Marinades

Marinades have a long history in outdoor cooking. Much of it has to do with the mixtures hiding the strong, gamey flavor of meats that did not receive proper care in the field. Marinade recipes commonly associated with wild game cooking almost invariably contain vinegar as one of the primary ingredients, as much to cover the flavor of the meat as for the marginal tenderizing effect it has.

Assuming that we are taking proper care of our game, let's look at marinades from another angle. Marinades differ from sauces in that they are applied to meats before the cooking begins rather than during or after. A marinade adds its flavor to the meat, then it is partially removed before or during cooking. Marinades containing a

*Bottled barbecue sauces are usually as good as anything
you can make from scratch.*

preponderance of vinegar will leave exactly that flavor with the meat
being prepared. Unless you're working with an old whitetail buck or
other tough, less than "Grade A"-quality game meat, you'll be better off
saving the vinegar for pickled fish.

There are as many marinade recipes as there are formulas for that
secret barbecue sauce. If you want to really keep it simple just soak
meat in any wine, with perhaps a shake of salt and pepper. Taking any
marinade recipe that has vinegar as an ingredient and replacing the
vinegar with an equal amount of wine will improve it. Figure white wine
for birds and fish and red for deer and other game. You may test the
Bouwman Theory of Marinade Improvement in the comfort of your

very own home, or camp, if you like, by taking a healthy swig of red and/or white wine, followed by a gulp of vinegar. Now, which did you enjoy more?

How long should meats remain in a marinade? Try to get them soaking a day ahead of time. This is not always possible, of course, but to get any benefit at all from the marinade figure at least eight hours for meats such as venison and small game, and at least half that for fish and birds. The temperature affects the speed with which a

Most venison dishes can be enhanced with the use of a marinade.

marinade penetrates the fibers of meat, with the marinating process speeding up as the temperature rises.

This recipe is a simple, all-around game meat marinade for small game, venison, or bear. Replace the red wine with white for birds.

Venison Marinade

2 cups red wine
1 cup water
1 teaspoon garlic powder
1 teaspoon pepper
1 bay leaf
$1/2$ cup salad oil

This next marinade is at its best when used with game ribs, cooked the way we did them in the over the open Fire chapter. This is Mike's recipe from deer camp.

Roeper's Rib Marinade

2 cups pineapple juice
1 cup soy sauce
3 tablespoons garlic powder
1 teaspoon cinnamon
2 teaspoons celery salt
1 green bell pepper, diced
2 teaspoons salt
3 teaspoons seasoned pepper

Chicken or Game Bird Marinade

$1/2$ cup vegetable oil (olive oil is best)
$1/2$ cup white wine
$1/2$ cup lemon juice
1/2 cup diced onion
$1/4$ teaspoon celery salt
$1/4$ teaspoon pepper
1 teaspoon garlic powder
$1/4$ teaspoon rosemary
$1/4$ teaspoon thyme

We used this next marinade in the Wok chapter. It is strong enough for coot. merganser, bufflehead, and other fish-eating ducks. Let these species spend a full day in the marinade, two is better.

Coot Marinade

1 cup water
1 cup red wine
$1/2$ cup soy sauce

Fish most often end up in the frying pan, and rightly so. Few meals can equal fresh-caught fish fillets, rolled in cornmeal and sputtering in hot oil next to a pot of baked beans. Try this for those fish that you don't want to fillet: bullheads and such. Use this marinade before baking fish in a reflector or Dutch oven.

Fish Marinade

1 cup salad oil
$1/4$ cup lemon juice
2 teaspoons tarragon
$1/2$ teaspoon thyme
$1/4$ teaspoon garlic powder

Just about any combination of lemon juice, white wine, and oil will do a good job on fish, including and especially the rough fish we discussed in the chapter on fish.

Are you strapped for time, or don't feel like fooling around with marinade recipes? A "universal" marinade that gives pretty good results on just about anything is plain old separating Italian salad dressing. Any one will do, but I'm partial to the dry mixes to which you add oil and water. These are an item that you can keep in your camp kitchen for those game meat windfalls that can be a featured item on the evening meal.

Basic Marinade Ingredients

Marinades are a rewarding, and mostly unexplored, area of camp cooking for many. If you want to work with some marinades during this year's camping season, here is a list of items to have in the camp kitchen:

Red wine
White wine
Soy sauce
Lemon juice
Salad oil
Pineapple juice (use the small, six ounce cans)
Tarragon
Thyme
Garlic powder
Cinnamon
Celery salt
Salt
Seasoned pepper
Rosemary
Bay leaf

Whether you carry all these ingredients will depend, of course on your situation. Sticking with small quantities, the permanent camper can keep a full stock of marinade ingredients in camp in very little space. This is a bit heavy for the pack or canoe. What you can do on those trips is carry a packet of the instant Italian salad dressing mix mentioned earlier plus a little salad oil.

12

Water

The Fox River rises in the sandy oak woodlot, scrub pine, and farm country of central Wisconsin. Snaking its way northeast across the state it forms two shallow, weed-choked bass and waterfowl lakes. Then it merges with the Wolf River to form Lake Winnebago which supports the largest population of lake sturgeon in the United States. It finally empties into Lake Michigan at the city of Green Bay. The Fox River is as temperamental and beautiful as a river can be, with the mad brown rush of its spring runoff melding into the more sedate pace of the summer flow, gathering and spreading and growing stronger with each mile.

By the time the Fox has reached that first shallow lake, however, the Wisconsin Department of Natural Resources advises anglers to eat bullheads in moderation, and northern pike and crappies not at all. Further downstream, as the river gathers paper mills and heavy industry along its banks, walleye, carp, and white bass are added to the list. This part of the Fox has the notoriety of being named in a national science magazine as the river where the fish have cancer.

PCBs, in this case. Polychlorinated biphenyls. Though not manufactured in the U.S. since 1977 they still haunt us, along with DDT, TCE, insecticides and other agricultural runoff, and a host of other substances. It was the cause of considerable confusion when I planned a Fox River canoe trip and looked into the question of water for cooking and drinking.

While one writer has recommended solving this type of problem by demanding fresh tap water from the offices of polluting industries along your route, my visions of river trips run more to the idyllic than the antagonistic, however just the cause. But as I gathered information on biological and chemical water pollution, the startling fact was not what was in the water, but how little most outdoorsmen know about it and how difficult it was to find lucid, reliable, and applicable information on the subject.

Daily Water Requirements

The moment the camper gets away from established camp- grounds with their faucets and well pumps, water takes on a new importance. The backpacker, back country big game photographer or hunter, and canoe tripper all must provide for a source of what makes up about one hundred pounds of your body weight. only the shortterm, vehicle-dependent camper can pack in enough water to meet his needs.

Depending on your physical activity, you need about a half gal- lon per day in a moderate climate, with that quantity doubling or more in a desert or arctic environment. At 50° F you can survive for about ten days without water, though this drops to a week when the temperature stands at 90° F and a mere two days at the desert tem- perature of 120° F.

Myths About Water Purity

Getting through a few of the myths surrounding water purity is the logical starting point for a look at drinking water for camp. No, drinking water from clear, rapidly flowing streams is not a safe practice. In fact, as we shall see later, taking raw water from exactly the opposite con- ditions is sometimes the best bet. A friend of mine likes to spend part of each September bowhunting elk in Colorado, where part of his wilderness experience was drinking directly from those clear, cold mountain streams. Until I told him that Bill, another friend who had drank from clear, cold mountain streams on a trout fishing trip had spent two weeks laying in bed recovering from his drink of water.

Another old one that still crops up is the myth of leaving water standing in sunlight for an hour to purify it biologically—that's another fine way to get sick.

Water Hazards: Bacteria, Viruses, Parasites and Chemical Pollutants

What exactly is in the water that is unhealthy to humans? Although a great deal of the problem is the result of our civilization fouling its own nest, disease organisms have been with us for some time, as indicated by a Smithsonian Institute researcher who reported in 1929 that the Chippewa Indians of Minnesota traditionally boiled drinking water when traveling away from home. Various bacteria, viruses, and parasites comprise the biological hazards facing the camper, while agricultural runoff of pesticides and herbicides and industrial dumping of organic compounds form the bulk of the chemical hazards in drinking water.

PCBs, dioxin, TCE, and a host of other acronyms and chemical names have become household terms for many Americans. Scientists admit that new problems in this area are surfacing faster than we can cope with the existing ones, so camp cooks can resign themselves to dealing with the problem of chemical pollution for the foreseeable future. Unlike treating biological hazards, dealing with chemical pollution will depend on your water source. While a mountain stream or marsh water that drains from a non-agricultural or industrial forest watershed can practically be considered chemically safe, rivers and lakes that escape industrial dumping usually receive runoff from farm fields.

The majority of these agricultural chemicals and industrial solvents are organic compounds. Toxic metals, such as lead or cadmium, can only be removed by distillation or other processes outside the abilities of the camper, and such waters should be avoided. By all means contact the conservation department in your state and find out who is dumping what and where. Ninety percent of the time it will be organic compounds, which can be dealt with as we will see when we discuss filtration.

Biological hazards include viruses, bacteria, and protozoans. Among the viruses, those causing hepatitis are the major players, though the disease is so rare in the United States (being primarily found in underdeveloped countries) that campers need not take any preventative measures. Bacterial hazards include strains of E. coli and

Salmonella, which are dealt with using the same measures as the greatest hazard of all to the camper, Giardia lamblia, the parasite responsible for giardiasis, or "beaver fever."

Giardia—The Camper's Nemesis

Giardia has been around for a long time—centuries, at least—but has only been recognized as a major problem for outdoorsmen in the last fifteen years or so. The parasite takes on two different forms during its life cycle: the trophozoite, which is the form that lives and breeds in the intestine of the host animal (you), and the cyst, an egglike structure that is eliminated from the host in the feces and lives in water until it is ingested by another mammal and can begin the trophozoite stage anew.

While enjoying the food, shelter, and hospitality of your intestine, the trophozoite will reproduce at a rate multiplying a single individual into one million parasites within ten days. Drinking as few as ten of the microscopic cysts can infect a human, presenting you ten days to two weeks later with diarrhea, abdominal cramps, fatigue, and perhaps vomiting and weight loss. Giardiasis persists for a week or two and is treated relatively easily by a physician. Though only about one fourth of those infected will develop symptoms, there is no way to tell ahead of time whether you belong to that lucky 75% that can live in harmony with Giardia lamblia.

Boiling Drinking Water

Now let's see what we can do to remove or neutralize these chemical and biological hazards so that we can take a drink of water. First, the original, fool-proof method: boil it for twenty minutes at sea level. This will kill viruses, bacteria, and parasites as well as or better than any other method, but is drastically time consuming and does nothing for any chemical contaminants, which brings us to water purification devices and chemicals.

Using Water Purification Tablets

First the chemicals, starting with the old sportsman's standby, Halazone tablets. Halazone releases chlorine—similar to household bleach—to disinfect water. The problem is that chlorine also reacts with any other organic material in the water, such as the small plant life found in water sources that would be tapped by the outdoor cook, reducing its effectiveness on bacteria and parasites. Its shelf life under optimum conditions is not the best, and drops to a mere five months if stored at 90° F. or above. Exposure to air reduces its potency about 75%, and on top of all that, chlorine just doesn't do a very good job of killing Giardia cysts.

Additional iodine is needed as the temperature drops.
Dosages are measured in capfuls.

Halazone has been replaced with iodine tablets, sold under the trade names of Globaline or Potable Aqua. Iodine in this form has a great shelf life—up to five years unopened at room temperature according to the manufacturer—and is effective against Giardia cysts.

The use of crystalline iodine, as opposed to tablets, avoids the risk of drinking contaminated water due to the reduced potency of air-exposed iodine tablets (which should be discarded sometime between three months and a year after exposure to air). I observed upon returning from a wilderness canoe trip that the bottle of Army surplus iodine tablets that I used was dated ten years prior to the month in which I was reading the bottle. I guess that either there were no Giardia cysts floating in my area during that week or that I'm one of those that isn't affected by the parasite. I bought my iodine tablets at the store after that, by the way.

Water Purifiction Systems

A crystalline iodine water purification system ideal for backpacker or canoe tripper is the Polar Pure, manufactured by Polar Equipment of Saratoga, California. It consists of a glass bottle containing a small amount of crystalline iodine, a mesh particle trap to retain the crystals in the bottle, a small thermometer on the side of the bottle with a graph to measure the iodine solution dosage (the colder the water temperature, the more solution is needed), and directions for use fused to the bottle so they can't wash or rub off. At a retail cost of around $9.00 and a capacity of purifying 500 gallons of water, you can't go wrong.

If you keep the Polar Pure bottle full of water the shelf life is indefinite. Though iodine does a better job than chlorine at low temperatures, its disinfectant action is drastically slowed, so allow two to three times longer than the recommended time on the bottle for chilled water.

Water purification filters are where the real confusion begins. The problem is that no filter removes every contaminant that concerns us here. Each manufacturer stresses what his particular product will remove, while downplaying what it will not.

There are three basic construction concepts of individual water purification filters which are utilized alone or in various combinations in the purification devices on the market. Iodine-impregnated resin filters are effective against many species of bacteria and viruses but are not considered by many authorities to be 100% effective against Giardia cysts. The claims made by manufacturers about these types of filters are disputed by some scientists, and I consider the question of their dependability to be subject to some reservation.

The silver infused activated charcoal filter is effective in removing larger particles and cysts (but not Giardia), and will effectively remove the organic compounds (agricultural runoff, PCBs, and so forth) that we discussed earlier, plus chlorine or iodine used to bacteriologically disinfect the water before filtering. The charcoal filter lets most biological hazards flow through, while the silver prevents bacterial growth within the filter when not in use.

The latest group of filters on the camper's market are the microstrainers. These filters have pores measuring .2 to .4 microns, effectively removing Giardia and other cysts, bacteria, and other particulate matter. A microstraining filter on its own will not remove chemicals, nor will it affect viruses in any way as there is no chemical treatment involved and a fat, healthy virus won't run much more than .06 of a micron or so, well under the pore size of the microfilter.

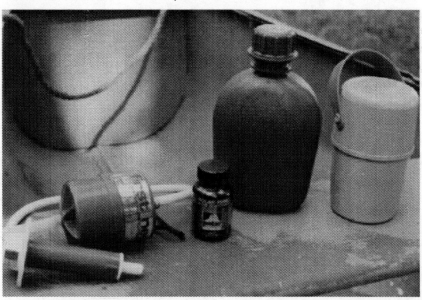

Water purification devices for camp include left to right, microstrainers, iodine treatments, and activated charcoal filters.

So which device or chemical is right for your application? First off, I have found little use for the iodide-impregnated resin filters. They do an incomplete job of removing chemical pollutants and particles and they are not 100% effective against Giardia, the primary health threat to the camper. You will likely want to end up with a system which utilizes both a filter and a chemical. The Portable Water Washer or Super Straw, both activated carbon filter units produced by Advanced Filtration Technology of Concord, California, do the same job in two

*The water system utilizes chlorine treatment
and an activated charcoal filter.*

different sizes. Discard the little bottle of chlorine that comes with each unit and replace it with the Polar Pure iodine solution and you have 100% bacterial disinfection, particle and debris removal, and chemical pollutant removal from your water supply.

At the time of this writing there are two microstraining units on the market, the $175.00 Swiss-made Katadyn, distributed by Provisions Unlimited of Oakland, Maine and the $35.00 First Need, manufactured by General Ecology. Inc. of Lionville, Pennsylvania. The Katadyn is probably the more durable of the two, being constructed of stainless steel versus the First Need's plastic, and contains a ceramic filter that strains particles to .2 micron. The First Need strains to .4 micron and contains in addition a charcoal filter to remove organic compounds. If there is any one device that is complete, the First Need is it. It does not protect against viruses, of course, but these are usually not considered a problem in the United States and precautions against them are usually not warranted.

Finally, what do you do if you have to have drinking water and you are without the means of purifying it? Boil it. Build a solar still if you are in the desert. At least drink from the cleanest looking source you can find. A guide in the Boundary Waters Canoe Area Wilderness tells me that most of his parties do not treat their water. He recommends drawing water from the centers of lakes or slow-moving rivers, as the heavier-than-water Giardia cysts tend to sink to the bottom. Fast-moving stream water keeps them agitated and suspended, reversing the pure-water-from-streams myth.

And the outfitter says not to take water downstream from beaver houses. Giardiasis has been called "beaver fever," as the big rodents spread the cysts by untidily defecating in and near the water. Interestingly enough, though, recent studies indicate that beavers located downstream from U.S. National Forest campgrounds show a higher rate of Giardia infection than do those in true wilderness areas. It may be that "beaver fever" is actually "human fever."

13

A Trip to the Grocery Store

Many of the best camp foods aren't packaged in foil pouches and sold in sporting goods stores. They're found on the shelves of your local supermarket. There is little need for you to pay inflated prices for identical items that say "camp" or "trail" on the package. The grocery store often can supply the ingredients for an entire outdoors meal from soup to dessert. And it also can supplement fish, game, and wild-plant foods to create some memorable camp meals.

I have a hunting and fishing buddy who has the unique talent of causing rain to fall whenever he pitches a tent. There's no black cloud hanging permanently over his head—unless he's hiding it under his hat—but according to my outdoor journal over the past few years it's 50% more likely to rain if he is along.

He was along on one trip I remember well. Surf casting along the Lake Michigan shoreline in April is a masochist's delight. You experience forty- degree water, the frothy tops of four- and five-foot waves blown in your face by the wind, the pounding of the surf against your legs for hours, and that occasional leap as a particularly tall wave claws for the top of your waders. It's wet and cold. Your clothing slowly fills with sand, and you have to shout all day to be heard over the roar of the big lake. The fishing is never crowded in the spring.

That evening found us back at camp without a single fish to show for our effort, and none of the three anglers present were up to any culinary exercise. After wet clothes, waders, and hot drinks were dealt with, a few boxes from the supermarket came out of the food crate. I remember a box of fettucini-style egg noodles, improved with a grating of cheese and a spot of wine and accompanied by a Dutch oven stew of canned chicken, dried mushrooms and dried, sliced potatoes, moistened with water and gravy mix. Maybe it wasn't such a bad trip after all.

And gameless or game-scarce meals can be enjoyed in equal style, and at a low price, whether you are camping with your vehicle or on a trip that demands space and weight restrictions such as living out of a canoe or pack. Dried beef, gravy base, a boxed rice or pasta side dish, and some dried fruits make up an entire meal for two for the cost of one pouch of a freeze-dried gourmet entree. The camping supply store food counters and mail order catalogs have their place in the outdoor foods market, and they do a good job of filling it. But a perusal of the corner grocery will feed you well and save money better spent on other gear.

Basic Classifications of Grocery-store Items

Grocery store foods can be loosely divided into convenience items (like soup mixes and macaroni and cheese) and staples (such as dried peas and beans). In between are peanut butter, dry meats and sausage, cheese, and a few other foods which don't seem to fit into either category.

Beverages

Probably the most familiar grocery store camp foods are beverage items. From coffee and tea, whether in leaf or bean form or as instant products, to fruit drinks, instant protein breakfast drinks, hot chocolate and the electrolyte replacement drink products such as Gatorade, the camp cook can do the bulk of his beverage shopping in the grocery store. While some of these products are packed in the individual portions preferred by the backpacker and canoe camper, most are bulk packed. One place to look for hard-to-find individual portion beverages, regular instant coffee and powdered coffee cream-er, for example, is at institutional food distributors in the larger cities. Many of these establishments provide a cash and carry department for walk-in customers, with a greater selection of products and prices eas-ier to live with than most mail- order camping supply houses.

Convenience Items

Some of the convenience items found in my camps include instant soups, gravy and sauce mixes, beverage powders, and a broad array of rice, noodle, and potato items that include a sauce mix in the box. While this last may bring to mind gruesome childhood memories of too much macaroni and cheese, most of them are edible, convenient to work with under poor weather conditions, and are inexpensive. With the addition of a little meat or fish they can serve as an entire meal in a pinch.

Just a few of the grocery store foods that
should come along on your next trip.

Gravy, Sauce Mixes and Soups

Gravy and sauce mixes and some of the instant soups are an essential part of the camp cook's pantry. I recall a deerless deer season when the most game I saw in camp was two squirrels. They were bubbling in a pot of water to which was added a few potatoes, an onion, and a package of gravy mix and one of soup. It didn't take tired hunters any longer than a few minutes here and there to prepare while completing the other end-of-the-day tasks, and I still remember the way it felt going down on a snowy night.

Stocking a well-rounded selection is not a problem due to the vast number of products on the supermarket shelves. Much of oriental cooking, with its roots in a fuel and meat-poor culture, is particularly suited to the dried meal in a box concept. I see more of these items offered all the time. From Chinese noodles to dried mushrooms to soup mixes, this is a good area to examine for the camp cook suffering from a jaded palate.

Puddings and other Desserts

Instant puddings and other related dessert items particularly hit the spot during cold weather, especially when youngsters are along. Producing a dessert is just the ticket for lifting literally dampened spirits during bouts of inclement weather. It's a real triumph over the elements to eat what some see as superfluous city food while the wind blows harder and the rain turns to sleet outside the tent.

Instant Breakfasts

Convenience grocery store chow really comes into its own at breakfast time. During the hunting season there just doesn't seem to be enough time to sleep. Instant oatmeal or other cooked cereals and some kind of dried fruit—apples, raisins, bananas, or whatever-doesn't eat up any more predawn time than making the coffee and is about as filling a meal as you can find. Instant oatmeal is sold conveniently packaged in single-serving packets, and with the addition of brown sugar and fruit it makes an excellent highcarbohydrate meal for cold weather activities.

Staple Foods

The staple foods from the supermarket are the foundations of your camp pantry. If you have dried beans, split peas, biscuit mix, cornmeal, and some rice in with your supplies you're carrying on a tradition of outdoor eating far older than you are. Add to that dry milk, a few varieties of pasta, some crackers and some dehydrated potatoes and you have a basic, weatherproof outfit that can stay packed with your gear year round serving as the foundation of a great deal of your camp cookery.

Your spices, of course, will come from the grocery store, but don't neglect dehydrated vegetables such as onions, chives, parsley, and green peppers that you will find in that department. These items provide a lightweight, easy-to-handle addition to stews, soups, or potato or rice dishes that just needs to be sprinkled in during the cooking process.

After the camp stove, I vote the ziplock bag the most important outdoor culinary breakthrough of the century. Repacking grocery

*Here is a selection of some grocery store foods that
adapt well to camp cooking.*

store food not only gets it into more durable and packable containers, to but allows you to bring only enough for your needs for a particular trip. It makes meal planning easy by allowing stew, soup, baking, or dessert items to be bagged together.

A simple one-pot meal, for example, can be a stew of dehydrated potatoes, vegetables, and beef jerky, portioned out with some gravy mix. There's no time wasted searching for ingredients at mealtimes, and your prepackaged entree will run you considerably less than its freeze-dried counterpart.

Peanut butter is impervious to summer heat and sub-zero winter temperatures alike, and primarily for this reason I keep some with our camp staples. It's good for you, high in energy, and fits just about any meal.

Meats

While bacon and sausage are always suitable for camp, some hold up without refrigeration better than others. The fall or winter camper can go the inexpensive route, but quality smoked bacon is called for as opposed to the usual packaged meat counter sugar cured variety if it will be exposed to the summer heat. Smoked bacon can be difficult to locate at the supermarket, but a call to a meat market or smokehouse will steer you to it. Any sausage found in non-refrigerated displays is suitable for camp provisions, and the smoked sausage in the meat counter will last for a considerable time if kept cool at night by storing in a stream or "wilderness refrigerator"—a canvas pack soaked with water and left to collect the night breezes.

other meat items that will serve the camp cook well are dried beef and ham, though expensive, and canned meat products such as beef slices, chicken meat, corned beef, and the best-known meat product of all, Spam.

Cheeses

Cheeses vary in their ability to lie outside the refrigerator. Anything goes during the cold season. During warmer weather, the rule is that the more "real" it is, the better. The farther away you stay from processed cheese spreads and their ilk the better your cheese will keep, and the closer it will resemble its original form when you pull it out of the pack at the end of the day. You don't have to stop at the gourmet shop to find a good cheese—cheddar, Monterrey Jack, colby, and so forth will do. Stay away from anything in a jar or with a color suitable for fire engines or deer hunting clothes and you'll be okay.

Recipes

Here are a few other creations from the shelves of the local grocery store that have worked out well in some of my camps:

Grocery Store Stew

1 package dried beef or a handful of jerky
1 large handful dried potatoes
Dried onion to taste
1 package beef gravy mix
Water

Soak the potatoes, onion, and jerky or dried beef. Add the rest of the ingredients, boil, and season to taste.

Supermarket Fried Rice

1 cup rice, cooked and drained
1 small package dried oriental mushrooms
Diced dry onion
Soy sauce
Any meat on hand (optional)

Drain the rice as completely as possible. one day old is best. Reconstitute the onions and mushrooms. Heat an oiled pan until smoking, add rice, and when it begins to brown sprinkle it with soy sauce and add the rest of the ingredients. This will serve equally well as a part or an entire meal.

Rice Pilaf

1 cup rice

2 cups water

$1/2$ of a chicken bouillon cube

1 package oriental dried mushrooms

1 tablespoon dehydrated onions

1 tablespoon dehydrated green pepper

1 teaspoon parsley flakes

Bring the water to a boil, add half a bouillon cube, add the rice, and bring the water back to a boil. Lower the heat to a simmer, add mushroom, onion, green pepper, and parsley. When the rice has absorbed all the water, serve.

14

Freeze-dried Camp Food

Only a whitetail doe and her twin fawns, a single loon, and the setting sun saw the two Voyageurs paddle the canoe around the beaver lodge and glide noiselessly to the beach. The first man stepped out of the birchbark craft and steadied it for the other. He pulled the canoe parallel with the shoreline and began unloading it as the second man leaned his flintlock rifle against a tree and gathered firewood.

They were tired and very hungry. The day's labor had planted in them an appetite that some men will never feel, and it was time to eat. A pack was opened and the makings of the evening meal were spread out on a rock as flames snapped and flickered from the pile of sticks set alight by the second man. The first man opened the foil packages of shrimp creole and beef stroganoff, added water, and asked his partner if he preferred spinach or green peas with his entree.

Beef stroganoff? of course we know that those daring Frenchmen who opened up the fur trade in North America lived on simpler fare than this. A diet of straight pemmican; a mixture of rendered animal fat, pulverized jerky, and berries, was standard fare in this period of history preceding the bean, bacon, and bannock period of North American camp cuisine. While complete nutritionally due to the dried berries, I guarantee that a steady diet of pemmican would send any present-day camper screaming in the direction of the nearest freezedried lasagna if eaten for three meals straight.

Freeze-dried Meals—A Boon for Novice Campers

The camp cook is currently bombarded with an array of freezedried foods. While I don't always feel right eating turkey tetrazzini out of a foil pouch when the loon laughter is in my ears and a northwoods sunset in my eyes, freeze-dried foods have a place in the camp kitchen. one that should be mentioned first is in the camp kitchen of the novice camper. The beginning backpacker or canoe camper pulls out of his or her driveway on Friday afternoon facing an awful lot of new experiences. For the novice, meal planning can be a real headache. Freeze-dried meals, a few simple cooking utensils, and a miniature camp stove can take the worry and hassle out of feeding your camp on a trip that requires the exercise of too many other skills, from properly planting the tent so you can enjoy a warm, dry night's sleep, to dealing with blistered feet or canoeing into a head wind.

From a catalog listing freeze-dried camp foods select your breakfasts, lunches, dinners, snacks and desserts. Use the portion guidelines we discuss later in this chapter, and off you go. It will cost you a few bucks, and there are other drawbacks we'll examine, but for that first trip or two the headaches saved are priceless.

Unlike the majority of dehydrated foods, freeze-drying (or vacuum sublimation) lies outside the scope of do-it-yourself projects. In this process food products, whether cooked or raw, are subjected to temperatures in the 50⁻ F range in a partial vacuum. The vacuum causes the water in the foods, now frozen into ice, to change to a vapor, which is withdrawn from the freeze-drying chamber leaving the finished, freeze-dried product.

Removing the water content from food to a level below five percent makes it unpalatable to insects, mold, and bacteria. Keeping oxygen from it by way of foil packaging gives it an almost unlimited shelf life. When you open a package you will have to use it within the foreseeable future—if not on the present trip then enjoy it at home.The water removed from freeze-dried foods reduces its weight by 90% and the bulk is decreased up to 90% in some, but not all, products. When reconstituted they will revive to something very close to their original form, and to a close facsimile of their original flavor.

Freeze-dried foods are a good choice for breakast—just add bread.

I personally find something lacking in the substance or "rib-sticking" quality of most freeze-dried foods. It just doesn't leave you with that proper post-prandial glow induced by a hunk of ban-nock dripping with the juices of fresh-picked blackberries. No bones to gnaw on and toss in the fire, I guess. This is, of course, an entirely subjective judgment, not unqualified but perhaps unjustified. others have voiced that same opinion to me, when asked, but a greater number look at me a bit funny and shake their heads. I have yet to do a blind tasting, comparing fresh food against its freeze-dried mirror image. It would certainly be illuminating one way or another.

Freeze-dried foods have made an undeniable impact on the camper's kitchen, but certainly not to the "revolutionary" extent claimed when they first appeared on the market. Folks were traipsing up and down mountain ranges and dipping canoe paddles while slapping mosquitoes long before things with names like vacuum sublimation appeared, so we must give the greater use of outdoor pursuits credit where credit is truly due: there's now more leisure time and money available to potential campers. Freeze-dried foods have an important and undeniable place in the practical camp kitchen, but let's also keep in mind that there are an equal number of places where they may not belong. Sometimes you need ten minute chicken ala king in camp, and sometimes you don't.

Advantages of Freeze-dried Meals

Like any specialized item of camping gear, freeze-dried foods have their pros and cons. on the pro side, they are cooked and preserved without, in the main, use of preservatives or additives (some outfits preserve the colors of apples and such with sulfites); they are as lightweight as you can possibly get in the arena of foodstuffs; with a few exceptions, the preparation of freeze-dried foods is so simple as to be practically idiot-proof; and they can provide services such as a hot, good-tasting meal to storm-bound travelers.

Disadvantages of Freeze-dried Meals

On the con side, they are expensive to the point of being twice the cost of conventional camp foods; they are known throughout the backpacking world for their bland, sometimes mushy taste; and last but definitely not least, remember that all that water that was taken out of your dinner by the manufacturer has to be put back in before you eat. If you are hauling water to a campsite, you can carry it whether still in your food, or, in the case of freeze-dried foods, separate in a canteen. one way or another, keep in mind that you are far from the sinks and faucets of home, and that freeze-dried foods may only be a sensible alternative if you have a water supply close to camp.

Freeze-dried Bulk Packaging

Freeze-dried foods are available in bulk packaging or, more commonly, portioned in one, two, or more single servings. The meal portions are designed for a race of campers that does not exist anywhere on earth, so be warned that they are unrealistic regarding feeding the advertised number of eaters. Multiply the manufacturer's recommendations by one and a half. In other words, a freeze-dried beef stroganoff meal for two will feed one person very well, and single servings need to be supplemented by an additional package. For winter camps, whitewater canoeing in cold weather, and other robust excursions where mealtimes get to be serious business you can figure two times the package recommendations.

Bulk foods such as diced pork, beef, or chicken, precooked hamburgers, scrambled eggs, vegetables, and fruits, are available in #10 sized cans. The cans have had their oxygen flushed and replaced with nitrogen, an inert gas that will not react with food products and cause spoilage. The bulk freeze-dried foods are mainly used for personal home emergency food storage programs.

Though you can save considerable money at first glance by buying bulk freeze-dried foods and repackaging them in portions for your next trip, remember that you are exposing the food to air whereby seeds of deterioration are planted. Such repacked foods should be used within the confines of the trip they are packaged for, or at home if another trip is not looming on the horizon. Removing bulk foods from the #10 cans carefully and slowly, so as not to disturb the nitrogen content of the cans and replace it with oxygen, will allow you to keep the open cans safely for use for an extended period.

If that last sounds vague, it is. Food deterioration begins the moment that the piece of plant or animal food dies, and continues, even if at an extremely slow rate of speed (as in the case of freezedried foods) until it has reduced itself to stable substances. All we can ever do is slow the process down. The process of deterioration depends on the amounts of heat, light, and moisture which reach the food product. The cooler, darker, and dryer your freeze-dried foods, or any other food products, are kept, the longer they will last and the better shape they'll be in when they are used.

Tips on Cooking Freeze-dried Foods

Cooking freeze-dried foods is a step up in the skill range from cooking canned foods, but a small step. From heat-and-eat we enter the world of add-water-and-stir. The raw freeze-dried products (uncooked scrambled egg mixes, for example) must be cooked by conventional camp means after being reconstituted from the freezedried state.

Here is a challenge for the camp cook—read and follow the package directions. If the instructions say to add one cup of boiling water, make sure that it is both one cup and boiling. Freeze-dried chow leaves little room for second-guessing the maker, and is not forgiving of errors. If the package demands cold water, do your best to find the coldest water you have on hand, though that can admittedly be difficult on the river in mid-June.

Cooking times are very important. You are receiving this food at the end of a long and complicated process of cooking and preserving. It has been abused about as much as it can take by the time it comes into your hands and cook pot, and that extra minute or so over the fire will reduce the already marginal substance of freeze-dried foods to something resembling all those little jars of chow you had around the house when the kids were still in diapers. Even a little too long on the heat will reduce any freeze-dried meal to mush.

Conversely, give it enough time. You have probably chewed on partially reconstituted dehydrated foods at one time or another if you have been camping long. Freeze-dried camp chow tastes just as chewy, stringy, lumpy, and tasteless if not more so than dehydrated foods.

Basic Spices Improve Freeze-dried Meals

Even if you're not a fan of overly spicy foods you will find many of the freeze-dried offerings to fall somewhere between bland and boring. While you can get by with salt, pepper, and a bottle of Tobasco sauce, packing the following away in plastic 35 mm film containers will give you the opportunity to vastly improve your culinary exercises in camp:

Chili powder   Curry powder
Oregano   Basil
Celery salt   Onion powder
Garlic powder   Parsley flakes
Rosemary (for pork and chicken dishes)
Beef and chicken base

Substituting Freeze-dried Ingredients

Cooking from "scratch" with bulk freeze-dried meats and vegetables, or the individually portioned diced chicken, beef, vegetables, and so forth available from most manufacturers, can be accomplished using any standard recipe, merely substituting freezedried ingredients for fresh or canned. Remember that you are dealing with reconstituted freeze-dried raw materials and not their fresh equivalent. Diced chicken will not take the handling abuse that you can subject fresh to without reducing itself to the fore-mentioned baby food consistency. Vegetables demand the same care. Any recipe in the line of a stew, the camp cook's favorite standby, can be used equally well with freeze-dried ingredients if you exercise a little care.

Another use for bulk freeze-dried meats and vegetables is to add bulk to prepackaged meals. A handful of diced beef added to the stroganoff or some vegetable to the stew can stretch a "serves two entree to the point that it actually does.

Cost Comparisons: Freeze-dried Vs. Grocery Store Foods

Every item produced for use in the outdoors has its "niche," from left-handed shotguns to waterproof note pads. And generally, the more specialized a product is the more it costs, without necessarily adding to the performance of its function. Thus while the freeze-dried entrees that feed Himalayan mountain-climbing expeditions and space shuttle drivers may be just the ticket for a rainy, rocky dinner on the lee side of an evergreen island during a northern Minnesota monsoon, the convenience and instant access offered by the freezedried food will hit you hard—in the wallet. The phrase "there ain't no such thing as a free lunch" could well have been born in the wake of a freeze-dried meal.

For the sake of this example we will use complete, packaged freeze-dried meals designed for two and divide the cost in half to look at what it will cost to feed one on a freeze-dried diet. (Though inflation may change these prices, the ratios will remain about the same.)

Breakfast:	Scrambled eggs	$3.18
	Hash browns	
	Applesauce	
	Cocoa	
Lunch:	Chicken salad	$3.80
	Biscuit	
	Pineapple chunks	
	Fruit punch	
Dinner:	Beef stew	$4.65
	Green beans	
	Strawberries	

Total cost: $11.63

Now let's take a look at a somewhat similar diet using inexpensive, somewhat lightweight foods packed from the home kitchen.

Breakfast:	Oatmeal with brown sugar	$.70
	Bannock with raisins	
Lunch:	Summer sausage	$1.95
	Cheese	
	Bannock with peanut butter	
	Homemade granola	
Dinner:	Rice with ham	$1.95
	Mashed potatoes with butter	
	Fresh carrots	
	Raisins	

Total cost: $4.60

As you can see, eating freeze-dried for a week's trip in the bush can add considerably to your fiscal responsibilities regarding camp eating.

When do you want to use freeze-dried camp foods? As we mentioned earlier, they have their niche. For long-range backpacking they can't be beat. The lighter your load, the more you will enjoy the trip. Extended canoe trips can also take advantage of freeze dried food, though more for its space-saving abilities than for the reduction in weight.

A couple of freeze-dried entrees tucked away in the bottom of the pack makes a good hedge against emergencies of all sorts, from merely being delayed a day or two due to inclement weather to a truly dangerous situation where a backwoods traveler may have to wait for rescue due to injury or loss of a canoe or wheeled transport. While I would be the last to promote taking to the woods with the goal of foraging 100% of your food supply for both practical, and in most cases, ethical reasons, it's fun to try under the right circumstances. A freeze-dried backup or complement makes a good time out of what could otherwise be a life and death situation when you're foraging.

Freeze-dried Recipes

The backpacker or canoeist can take advantage of combining fresh, natural gathered foods with some freeze-dried ingredients and throw together some fabulous meals far from civilization without dragging along the weight and bulk of one of your field kitchens. Using freeze-dried ingredients, like the vegetables mentioned earlier, fish and game recipes that call for stew ingredients or Chinese style wok-cooked dinners can be produced. Like these:

Wok Game Bird
1 bird (grouse, pheasant, duck, etc.)
1 4-ounce package (reconstituted) freeze-dried green beans
1 4-ounce package (reconstituted) freeze-dried peas
1/4 teaspoon garlic powder
Black pepper

Cooking oil
1/4 cup soy sauce
1/4 cup water
1 teaspoon cornstarch

Mix the water, cornstarch, and soy sauce before you leave home and carry in a leak-proof container. Clean and boil the game bird, and remove the meat from the bones. While cooking the bird, reconstitute the freeze-dried vegetables according to package directions. Heat oil in the wok to smoking, and add garlic powder. Add pieces of bird and vegetables, cooking rapidly over a hot flame and cooking the items separately if using a small pan. Do not over-cook—you want ingredients to be heated through only, remaining as crisp as possible. Add the corn-starch, water, and soy sauce mixture to coat the meat and vegetables well. Stir them, and remove from heat. Season with the pepper.

Some foraged mushrooms or acorns make great additions to your wok dinner.

Backpacker's Fish Chowder

Fish—a carp, bullheads, mess of small panfish, or
    whatever, cleaned and cut into chunks
1 8-ounce package (reconstituted) of freeze-driedcorn
4 cups milk, made from dry milk
1 cup instant mashed potatoes
1 tablespoon margarine
1/2 of a chicken bouillon cube, crushed
1/2 teaspoon celery salt
1/2 teaspoon onion powder
Salt and pepper

Bring the milk almost to a boil. Add the fish, corn, potatoes, and margarine. Add the rest of the ingredients and simmer for half an hour. Add more bouillon cubes if additional seasoning is required.

15

Cans and Retorts

The origin of Food Preservation in Bottles and Cans

As is the case with much of our current technology, the development of canned foods can be attributed to mankind's predilection for warfare. As Napoleon's armies ravaged and burned their way back and forth across Europe, his soldiers suffered the fate of all military expeditions of that period: nutritional deficiencies caused by a limited diet of smoked fish, salted meat, and hardtack. The French government offered a reward for a method of preserving foods without refrigeration, and in 1790 paid that reward to Nicolas Appert, who developed a method of sealing food in glass containers and boiling the bottle.

An American, Thomas Kensett, developed the metal can for preserving food, and by 1850 the mass-produced, stamped metal can was in wide use—just in time for the American Civil War. The two opposing armies did a more thorough job of exposing Americans to different varieties of food that any present-day Madison Avenue advertising agency could ever hope to, sending the survivors home with a decided taste for canned food.

The can was a natural for outdoor life, though that life at the time leaned more towards vocations than vacations. Canned food in camp was a welcome addition to the beans, bacon, and bannock school of cooking, adding variety that at one time could only be found upon returning home or to some facsimile of civilization. The can was firmly entrenched in camp life, though it has lost considerable ground in recent times.

When you think backpacking, immediately the image of spaceage, foil-pouched freeze-dried meals comes to mind. Yet when I flipped on the radio the other day at the beginning of an interview with back-packers setting off on the long Appalachian Trail, the immediate answer to "What do you carry along to eat?" was "Canned chicken, smoked oysters, a six-pack of beer, you know. I try to avoid anything you have to add water to."

Spoken like a true long-time backpacker. While the freeze-dried outdoor food revolution has made long-range backpacking and canoe trips possible without mid-point provisioning of some sort, the word is out that while the freeze-dried gourmet meals hold a definite and secure place in the camp pantry, a steady diet of the stuff is more than most of us can stomach.

There is no way to tell how many of the twenty-six billion cans and jars of food consumed in the United States each year are eaten around campfires. The old canned camp staples, butter and bacon, have been replaced in the main with freeze-dried substitutes. These two items were about the only ones produced specifically for the camp kitchen, other canned foods being gleaned from grocery stores.

Avoid Hauling Water-heavy Foods in Cans

Canned foods fit well into different camp kitchens depending mostly on what type of camp we are considering. Notwithstanding the tongue-in-cheek remark of the Appalachian Trail backpacker we mentioned earlier, most backpackers avoid hauling water-heavy foods (like six-packs of soda pop) whenever possible. Some canned foods do well in the pack however, such as ham, chicken, turkey, and fish products in smaller, single-serving-sized cans. These items contain relatively little water for their bulk, as compared to a canned vegetable or fruit, for instance, and take up little space in the pack. A further advantage over their freeze-dried equivalents is that in an emergency or a quick trail stop there is no need to start a fire or stove and no extra water is required.

Temperature and Shelf-life Concerns

Canned goods do need to be protected from extremes of temperature. They will survive one freezing without too much damage, but use the contents immediately, right from the frozen state, as you will have an unpalatable mess once they thaw in the can.

The shelf life of canned foods varies widely depending on who you consult, but consider one year to be the very maximum. Canned foods begin to lose their nutritional value and flavor from the moment they hit the bottom of the can, and after spending a year in there they should come out of the camp kitchen and be used up in the home.

There isn't a whole lot to say about the actual cooking in camp of canned foods as this step has been done for you by the manufacturers as part of the canning and labeling process. Cooking canned foods is simply a matter of heat and eat. Soups and stews made in camp can benefit from the use of the liquid in the can in the cases of canned vegetables or meats, however. This liquid, which the contents of the can was cooked in during the canning process, is a stock, which we discussed in the chapter on sauces and gravies, and can be used for a base for sauces and soups.

The Retort Pouch

There is a new can in camp. The retort pouch, or Softcan as it is called by one manufacturer, retains the ready-to-eat advantage of canned food, while successfully dealing with the disadvantages of excessive bulk and very limited shelf life.

The "retort" of retort-pouch foods refers to the container in which the product is cooked after being packaged. The pouches differ radically from the traditional can in that they are constructed of an inner layer of polypropylene, an inert material that actually touches the food; a second layer of aluminum foil which provides a light and air barrier; and a tough outer layer of polyester to protect the first two layers.

Raw food is placed in the retort pouch during manufacture and cooked in the pouch, the same as canned foods are cooked in the can. The difference with the pouch is that due to its thinner shape, as compared to a can, less cooking needs to be done to bring the food to sterilization temperatures. This results in a more palatable product. The cooked food comes into contact with the polypropylene inner liner of the pouch as opposed to the metal of a can. This factor, and the fact that almost all of the air is removed from the pouch, is the reason for the longer shelf life of retort-packed foods. Yurika Foods claims a shelf life of two to five years. Van Rich, Inc., manufacturer of Smokey Canyon Softcan foods, claims a two-year shelf life. And the military, which has recently switched from the can to the pouch for field rations, says that its retort pouch foods have a shelf life of a little over eight years at 70° F. Research is still in progress as to how long the things will last, and time, quite literally, will tell.

Like any other canned foods, preparing a retort-pouch meal consists of heating and eating. The pouch has advantages over the can— it need not be opened nor have vent holes punched in it for escaping steam. That procedure must be followed when heating cans or the camp cook will end up at best experiencing the excitement of an exploding can and at worst wearing part of a blazing hot dinner.

The retort pouch is thin enough to be heated against the body or on an engine block if need be, and heats in boiling water very rapidly compared to cans due to its thinner configuration. It also burns (though you need a good hot fire to consume it completely), saving you the trouble of hauling the empties back to town.

Prices between retort camp foods and their freeze-dried equivalents are about equal. A quick perusal of mail-order catalogs shows single portions of retort-pouch beef stroganoff from two different manufacturers at $2.79 and $3.85 and a double portion in freezedried form for $5.49.

Limitations of Metal-can Food Preservation

Retort meals score quite well from a nutritional point of view, while standard canned food items don't do as well. The heat required for metal and glass container canning destroys much of the vitamin content of the foods. Also, quantities of salt and sugar must be added, in addition to other food preservation additives, in order to retain some of the original quality of the food.

*The camp cook that travels light but still makes use of some
canned foods will appreciate the P-38 can opener.*

One final strike against the can is the can itself. First, you need a tool to open it. While any can opener will do the job, the tool that is just made for camp is the G.I. issue P-38 can opener. This is a really neat little tool, and it actually works quite well. You will have to use it before you believe that last statement, because at first sight it just does not seem like a good idea. Also known as the "John Wayne," they are regarded by some who should know as perhaps the only worthwhile thing produced by the military.

Secondly, after eating canned food, you still have the can. Burn it out, if you are using a fire, to remove the remaining food residue from the inside of the can. Then flatten it with a size twelve or whatever you can muster, and pack it out.

Some voices within the food industry predict the total demise of the metal can. As more and more institutional products, from coffee to meats, are being marketed in various types of plastic pouches, the heavy, expensive metal can may eventually go the way of salt pork in a wooden barrel.

16

G.I. Food in Camp

It was one of the finer float trips of the year. Water levels were perfect on the Yellow River, a fickle wilderness stream burbling through the cut-over expanse of northern Wisconsin's pine and aspen woodlands. There was just enough rolling white water to exhilarate but not enough to force a portage, and the perch and walleye pools at the foot of each rapids were full and fat and calm. The fishing went well, the weather was cool enough for good sleeping under canvas and the rain held off.

It was probably the least-planned trip of the year. A Friday morning attack of office fever, a phone call, the frantic piling in the pickup of the aluminum canoe, tent, fishing gear, and food. If I was going to be on the water as soon as possible, that evening, no fooling around with menu planning or trips to grocery stores was allowed. A box in the garage held a number of brown, plastic bags—the latest in military field rations—and with a handful of these and a frying pan, a bag of cornmeal, and a little shortening to deal with any fish, I was off.

Browsers of sporting goods stores and mail order catalogs these days are overwhelmed by the quantity of olive drab or camouflage pattern "military surplus" equipment offered. From clothing to sleeping bags to knives, many of these items have a definite place on the sportsman's back or in his camp, though the vast majority isn't "surplus" anything, but are newly manufactured items conforming to current military appearance.

Though military rations would seem to symbolize the opposite pole from the kind of eating we're working on in this book, they do have a valuable, though limited, application for the camper, hunter or fisherman, and canoe tripper. As we have noted, the term "surplus" as applied to the sporting goods market is usually inaccurate. True government surplus consists of items that have been purchased by the military or some other government entity, either used or stored until they reach the end of the term of whatever shelf life the particular agency has assigned them, and then are sold. Field rations are not sold as surplus by the military. Those sold to sportsmen are products manufactured for the private sector after government contracts are fulfilled.

Types of Military Rations Available

Rations that you may encounter include the famous (or infamous, if you've been in the service) C-ration (for "canned" or "combat" ration). Its recent replacements are the MRE (or "Meal, Ready to Eat"); the MRE's cousin the LRRP, (or "Long Range Reconnaissance Patrol" ration); and to a much lesser degree, Civil Defense canned biscuits and various lifeboat or aircraft survival rations. These last two items usually will be actual surplus—used goods that have exceeded their storage life.

Use of the C-ration has been phased out by the military (mercifully, I'm told by veterans of my acquaintance), but will appear on the market from time to time as old manufacturers' stocks are depleted and due to new manufacture for foreign governments. The square box contains various canned foods, from main course items like Brunswick stew or beans and meatballs to accouterments and accompaniments such as jellies, peanut butter, fruitcakes, hot cocoa mix, cheese spread, instant coffee, sugar, a plastic spoon, and a token swatch of toilet paper. The box is about three by five by six inches and weighs almost two pounds. Not backpacker's food.

The MRE contains roughly the same quantity and type of foods, the difference being the retort pouch packaging which replaced the steel cans of the C-ration. The square box has given way to a tough plastic pouch measuring about eight by five by two inches. and weighing in at just over a pound.

The MRE is a lot easier to handle than the C-ration. Food can be eaten cold or the pouches heated as is in boiling water without worrying about bulged or exploding cans. The packaging makes it easier to fit into a pack or pocket, and puncturing the outer bag and squeezing the air out makes it more compact still.

Military surplus food is of comparable quality to commercial brands.

The LRRP ration is similar in packaging and content to the MRE, the difference being that the majority of the foods contained in it are freeze-dried. There is a corresponding decrease in weight. This ration was never produced in any great quantity, and is not seen on the market with the frequency of the other two field rations.

All of these meals are designed to provide adequate, balanced nutrition for individuals working under strenuous conditions. The quality is comparable to commercial canned or freeze-dried food. If you like canned spaghetti, you'll love military issue chow.

Advantages of Using G.I. Rations

The advantage of using Cs or MREs for certain applications is that you have a complete meal in one package, spoon and all. While the C-ration, with its tin cans, is pretty much relegated to the car camper or the veteran looking for a fond reminiscence of days past, the MRE fits neatly into an outdoor niche or two. Use some water to reconstitute the few freeze-dried and dehydrated items that these contain, and a container if you want to heat MRE pouches, and you're all set. Besides the impromptu canoe trips outlined at the beginning of this chapter, the day-trip backpacker or elk or deer hunter who wants either a hot lunch in the field or an emergency ration to be carried in case of an unplanned overnight stay in the bush may appreciate the virtues of G.I. food.

The solo elk hunter is a good candidate for a military surplus meal.

Disadvantages of Using G.I. Rations

The primary disadvantage of these meals is cost. At the time of writing these meals are in the five to six dollars apiece range, about twice

A small stove and one bag—a complete meal for the hunter or hiker.

the cost of duplicating their contents in the grocery store. Several companies are in the business of purchasing large quantities of the MRE rations from government contractors, however, so we can presume that these will become more available and at reduced prices in the future. Components, however, ranging from entree pouches of Chicken ala King to desert items like cakes or brownies, can be found at reasonable prices and make a good choice for some outdoor applications.

Campers interested in somewhat kinky culinary field exercises can send to the McIlhenny Company, makers of Tabasco sauce, for a Charlie Ration Cookbook or MRE Cookbook which will instruct you in the art of preparing entrees with names like Patrol Chicken Soup and Ham Grenades. Though hardly inspired cooking, the two booklets do

The MRE can be the answer for improvisioning impromptu canoe trips.

a neat job of demonstrating what can be done with a limited number of food items and, of course, a little Tabasco sauce.

Civil Defense biscuits and surplus survival rations have a lesser place in the outdoorsman's military food pantry. Week-long fishing or hunting camps will find the giant cans of biscuits handy and durable. And cheap. The price is right on these, and you can throw a can or two in the garage with the tent and not worry about them spoiling.

The aircraft and lifeboat rations consist of foil or poly-bagged candy and sometimes vitamin tablets. I would imagine the vitamins are long dead from the length of storage time, but the ration makes a neat, waterproof package to tuck into your pack or pocket along with space blanket and fire starter for the unexpected night in the woods.

Whether used to resurrect the traditional hunter's midday lunch and campfire in the field, or for providing a quick and reliable food supply for spur-of-the-moment weekenders, military rations have a place, though limited, in the outdoorsman's pantry.

Index